THE INTELLIGENT READER'S GUIDE TO READING

HOW TO READ A BOOK THE RIGHT WAY FOR
STRONGER COMPREHENSION AND BETTER
RECALL

THINKNETIC

CONTENTS

Your 60 Second Review Can Change Everything For Us

Whether you've just picked up this book or have already started reading, we'd love it if you could take just 1 minute to leave a quick review. It's as easy as scanning the QR code or following the short link below.

Your feedback—whether it's about the book's topic or your excitement to dive in—is incredibly important for us. Reviews not only offer us valuable feedback, but they also play a big role in shaping how this book reaches a broader audience.

If you'd like to go the extra mile, consider attaching a photo of the book—whether it's the cover or a glimpse of the content—making your review stand out to other readers.

Your review, even with just a few words and a quick photo, makes a world of difference. Thank you for being a part of this journey!

Christoph M.   *Michael M.*

Founders of Thinknetic

Go to: t.ly/tirgtrr

Get 100% Discount
On All New Books!

Get ALL our upcoming eBooks for FREE
(Yes, you've read that right)
Total Value: $199.80*

You'll get exclusive access to our books before they hit the online shelves and enjoy them for free.

Additionally, you'll receive the following bonuses:

Bonus Nr. 1

Our Bestseller
Critical Thinking For Complex Issues
Total Value: $9.99

Are you tired of being manipulated by fake news and false arguments?

Arm yourself with the ultimate weapon - critical thinking.

Critical Thinking For Complex Issues is your guide to cutting through the noise and discovering the truth.

Learn how to spot logical fallacies, overcome confirmation bias, and analyze arguments objectively.

"Before this book, I kept falling for online rumors. Ugh! This book explains critical thinking in a way that's super easy to follow. Now I can easily tell what's real and what's fake. Bonus: I learned how to have good conversations, not just pointless arguments. This book is awesome!"

Yvonne - Reviewed in the United States on June 13, 2024

"This short (~300 pages) guide offers a timely challenge to become better thinkers by identifying mental pitfalls that even the best of us can fall into, and how to avoid them. Beginning with an overview of the value of critical thinking in our modern world, the guide then introduces the Socratic approach to asking questions, followed by a discussion on Rhetoric (creating a persuasive argument)."

Thomas Jerome Newton - Reviewed in the United States on July 2, 2024

"This book really helped me to not put trust in everything we might read or hear. Actually it helped me to see how valuable it is to question everything I read and hear. Look at the source, agenda of the information, biased or unbiased etc. Excellent read!"

Jared Szalkiewicz - Reviewed in the United States on June 25, 2024

"This book is very well written which makes it an easy read for those who choose to stray away from the normal path of what I would call herd thinking. Very insightful and provocative. I have already recommended this as a must read to my network of friends and family."

Paul Shelton Sr. - Reviewed in the United States on June 20, 2024

Bonus Nr. 2

Our Bestseller
The Intelligent Reader's Guide To Reading
Total Value: $9.99

Ever feel like you've read a book but can't remember a single thing about it?

You spend hours pouring over pages, only to walk away with a vague sense of what you've consumed.

Imagine reading and actually remembering key arguments. Imagine truly understanding the author's message and discussing it with confidence.

This guide is your secret weapon.

"This is by far the best set of tools and strategies that I've read on improving reading. This is what I wished had been taught in Junior High. I've learned them by trial and error and see how they all fit together."

Michael McFarren - Reviewed in the United States on January 26, 2023

"It's been many years since I've started to regularly read books that I believe would help me grow. A challenge in doing so has been not having a systematic/strategic framework that will help me gain the most out of a book I've read. I'm glad to have found and read this, and after applying some techniques that I have learnt from this book, I already started to experience better results from my reading. I'm sure it will help you the same if you have similar challenge like I did.
Thanks to Thinknetic and its team for their good work!"

Sai Aung Lynn - Reviewed in the United States on April 23, 2023

"This book is very much practical. Straight to the point and concise. Comes with a lot of useful examples to build skills."

Amazon Customer - Reviewed in the United States on December 1, 2023

"I have read books of all types of genres for years. This book has clear and procise ways of reading to help one gain the most benefit out of their reading experience. I recommend all give it a good look there is something to learn for all."

Raymond E. Smith - Reviewed in the United States on March 2, 2023

Bonus Nr. 3 & 4

Thinking Sheets
Break Your Thinking Patterns
&
Flex Your Wisdom Muscle
Total Value Each: $4.99

A glimpse into what you'll discover inside:

- How to expose the sneaky flaws in your thinking and what it takes to fix them (the included solutions are dead-simple)
- Dozens of foolproof strategies to make sound and regret-free decisions leading you to a life of certainty and fulfillment
- How to elevate your rationality to extraordinary levels (this will put you on a level with Bill Gates, Elon Musk and Warren Buffett)
- Hidden gems of wisdom to guide your thoughts and actions (gathered from the smartest minds of all time)

Here's everything you get:

✓ Critical Thinking For Complex Issues eBook **($9.99 Value)**
✓ The Intelligent Reader's Guide To Reading eBook **($9.99 Value)**
✓ Break Your Thinking Patterns Sheet **($4.99 Value)**
✓ Flex Your Wisdom Muscle Sheet **($4.99 Value)**
✓ All our upcoming eBooks **($199.80* Value)**

Total Value: $229.76

Go to the end of the book for the offer!

*If you download 20 of our books for free, this would equal a value of 199.80$

WHAT READERS ARE SAYING ABOUT THINKNETIC

"I wanted to read some books about thinking and learning which have some depth. I can say "Thinknetic" is one of the most valuable and genuine brands I have ever seen. Their books are top-notch at kindle. I have read their books on learning, thinking, etc. & they are excellent.

—*Sahil Zen, 20 years old from India, BSc student of Physics*

"Thinknetic's works provide a synthesis of different books giving a very good summary and resource of self-help topics. I have recommended them to someone who wanted to learn about a topic and in the least amount of time."

—Travvis Mahrer, BA in Philosphy, English Teacher in a foreign country

"I have most of the ebooks & audiobooks that Thinknetic has created. I prefer audiobooks as found on Audible. The people comprising Thinknetic do an excellent job of providing quality personal development materials. They offer value for everyone interested in self-improvement."

—Neal Cheney, double major in Computer-Science & Mathematics, retired 25yrs USN (Nuclear Submarines) and retired Computer Programmer

"I came to know about Thinknetic from the Amazon Kindle. There were recommendations for some of the Thinknetic books. Found every book very interesting. I really loved it. Subscribed for the free material which was delivered right into my inbox. Since then, I have been a fan. I couldn't buy the books... since am in a situation. But as soon as I get a sufficient amount, I plan to purchase some nice titles that piqued my interest. I recommend the books to everybody who wants to live a life free from all sorts of mental blocks that reflect in real life. These books are definitely the lighthouse, especially for those crawling through the darkness of ignorance. I wish Thinknetic all the best."

—Girish Deshpande, India, 44, Master of Veterinary Science, working as an Agriculturist

"Thinknetic embodies an innovative and progressive educational approach, expertly merging deep academic insights with contemporary learning techniques. Their books are not only insightful and captivating but also stand out for their emphasis on practical application, making them a valuable resource for both academic learning and real-world personal development."

—*Bryan Kornele, 55 years old, Software Engineer from the United States*

"I've been working my way through the Thinknetic books. It's been a couple months now, and I'm enjoying exploring new ideas and new ways at looking at things. I think these books are helpful for anyone who wants to improve their thinking skills, particularly in business settings. They're also an option for people who are just generally interested in self-improvement."

—Drew Del, Hawaii (USA), 48, Post-grad cert in Education, works as Entrepreneur & Researcher

"I have been reading books from Thinknetic for a while now and have been impressed with the CONDENSED AND VALUABLE INFORMATION they contain. Reading these books allows me to LEARN INFORMATION QUICKLY AND EASILY, so I can put the knowledge to practice right away to improve myself and my life. I recommend it for busy people who don't have a LOT of time to read, but want to learn: Thinknetic gives you the opportunity to easily and quickly learn a lot of useful, practical information, which helps you have a better, more productive, successful, and happier life. It takes the information and wisdom of many books and distills and organizes the most useful and helpful information down into a smaller book, so you spend more time applying helpful information, rather than reading volumes of repetition and un-needed filler text.

"Thinknetic provides excellent thought provoking and incisive books. They have a high rate of turnout and I am glad they have started doing audio books. I recommend their books to anyone wanting to improve themselves young or old. You are never too old to learn."

INTRODUCTION

Do you know how to read?

You might scorn this question instantly, since, well, you are technically reading it. And you're right to do so if you consider that the inquiry is about your literacy. It is not! This question has so many layers that it deserves to have a whole book written about it. Let us envision this scenario:

You just read the last page of a book, closed it, and a feeling of exhilaration fills you up. You are so excited that you pick up the phone, and call your best friend telling them excitedly, "I have just finished the most brilliant book ever written!" Your friend, who gets thrilled at the sound of your voice, asks, "Really? What's it about?"

Your smile starts to fade as you stumble, trying to create a comprehensible sentence. The ideas of the book are floating in your mind; you remember clearly the instances that mesmerized you. But how do you explain that feeling? How can you relay in words and convince your friend that this is the book of the century?

You start by telling them the ideas. You talk about the way the writer brilliantly described a particular instance. You then remember that for them to understand how powerful that description was, they need to know something else that occurred prior to that. You then try to explain it again with the background information. You suddenly recall an exceptionally well-written paragraph that they must know about. Maybe they'd understand better. You fumble through the pages of the book as you speak, excitedly trying to look for that part that will help them understand. You start to lose their interest.

"Yeah, that sounds really good, I guess," you'd hear them say unenthusiastically. You feel disappointed, why couldn't they understand? Why couldn't you explain how good it was? You just end up saying, "Well, you should read it; it really is brilliant!"

This happens maybe more often than many of us care to admit. Or maybe, you just finished a book and felt that the writer could have done a better job, but you could not pinpoint the exact reason behind your feeling. In some instances, you might have read about a complex idea or concept and found that it would fit perfectly in a conversation you're having with your coworkers. But you just couldn't explain it well enough to get the conversation going.

Have you always wanted to be an intellectual who understands economics, politics, philosophy, and psychology? Were you ever curious to read and fully understand the theories of Confucius, Immanuel Kant, or Simone de Beauvoir? Do you want to know what the greatest minds of our species thought and created, and you realize that books are the window to take a peek?

Reading isn't only about the ability to decipher words on paper; it surpasses the ability to learn our ABCs. Reading is an art that we need to perfect to make the most of our development, and learn about the world and everything in it. Regardless of what we would like to improve within ourselves, it all starts with our brains. And reading is the exercise of the mind. We read to learn, we read to evolve, and we read to expand our horizons. Does knowing your ABCs suffice to achieve such major goals?

This book was compiled to help readers move beyond reading words and sentences. It takes its readers on a step-by-step journey to help them dissect a book, understand it, and close it with a sense of fulfillment as the concepts and the ideas within are fully comprehended. You should finish reading a book, understand what's within, and end up with a clear opinion of your own regarding the topic it discusses.

This book aims to assist the reader in considering alternative ways of reading other than just opening a book and reading it cover to cover. Even if you aren't specialized in the particular field you are reading about, you do have the intellectual capacities to benefit the most from reading and understanding the main concepts of a book regardless of how difficult they are. You only lack the tools that help you make use of your intellect.

This is a guide that builds up gradually to help you read better. However, it would almost be useless without you taking action on your part. You are a major component of its success in achieving its goal. What you do with the information within is as crucial as the ideas it contains. There will be exercises at the end of each chapter to help you apply the key concepts, which are cumulative as you make progress from one chapter to the next. Reading is a mental exercise, and if the reader does not take action and make the mental effort needed when reading this book, not much use will come out of reading it.

These pages are written by someone who loves to read, and always strives to read better and make the most out of good books they come across. We only hope that you find it an enjoyable read as much as it was a joy to write. If you are ready to make the most out of the books you read, this is a good place to start. So we ask again, would you like to know how to read? Well then, read on.

Wedad Naji Khoder

1

ARE BOOKS USELESS IN A DIGITAL WORLD?

WHY READING IS SUCH AN ESSENTIAL SKILL IN OUR MODERN TIMES

Why Would I Read?

As Marie is cleaning the house, she sees her twelve-year-old sitting on the couch with his iPad playing games. She sighs as she prefers him to do something more useful and says:

"Just drop that iPad, John, and go pick up a book to read."

"But it's summertime! I can't believe I'm done with school, so why would I read?" complains John.

"Well, reading is fun. Besides, it will be good for you."

"Why would it be? I've had enough reading in school. Why should I read?"

"Well… because… it is good for you!" repeats the mother hesitantly as she tries to think of a more convincing answer.

"Yeah, but why? You all say it is good for me. How is it good for me?"

"Well, you'll be able to gain knowledge that the iPad definitely doesn't have!" she replies confidently.

"But Mom, I have the Internet on the iPad. I can learn anything I want. Why should I read a book?" he replies sarcastically.

Marie knows that her boy is trying to outsmart her to get out of picking up a book and reading. She doesn't know how to convince him that reading is much more useful than going online. She knows that reading is good. But she starts pondering on his questions. Why indeed should he read? And how is it good for him? As she starts considering the questions, she gets angry and replies:

"Fine, suit yourself. But it is your loss, you know!" She goes about doing her chores angrily, thinking more about his questions.

Maybe, just like John and Mary, many of us wonder why it is so important to read. And we might also be wondering if reading is truly necessary. Since you have already picked up a book to read – a book about reading nonetheless – then most probably you believe that reading is important, just like Marie does. But if you're trying to explain why it is important, you might be at a loss too.

<u>Reading In The Digital World</u>

Our age is dubbed the Age of Information, and the Internet has changed numerous aspects of our daily lives.

It changed the way we receive information and the way we interact, and it created daily new habits altogether. This difference of opinion between Mary and John can be seen in every household, and it is a difference witnessed in every aspect of our lives, not just in reading. It might be difficult to imagine if there has been a society at any point in history where we've had such a huge gulf between the young and old [1].

When a mother like Mary tries to argue with her twelve-year-old about something such as the importance of reading, this gulf between the different perceptions shines through. And John does have a point, actually. Why read to gain knowledge? We now have the Internet. In that little gadget in our pockets, we have all of the information we might ever need to know. So why take the time to read a book? Besides, come to think of it, if I pick up a novel to read, for instance, what information might I gain? In contrast, I can go online and get way more information in a matter of minutes.

We must here differentiate between two kinds of thinking processes that are at the core of this debate: analytic thought and contemplative thought. Analytic thought is goal-directed and transitive. When thinking analytically, the information we seek is the means and the building blocks toward explaining something. And the Internet, which can compile and categorize data, is a powerful tool for such an end goal, no doubt.

Contemplative thinking, on the other hand, is in its nature, experiential and intransitive. The end goal of thinking contemplatively is reflection, and it is used as a means of experimenting and refining our relation to the world. When we contemplate, we are pursuing the satisfaction of being illuminated and gaining new insight. Gaining information in contemplative thinking is the mere context and not the end goal. When you take the time to read a book, you contemplate what it says, gain insight, and understand more about the world. Information happens to come along with the experience.

Analysis and contemplation are two opposite kinds of thinking. Depending on how they are used, the Internet and the book have also become opposites in this sense [2]. Of course, the Internet can be used to gain insight and think contemplatively about a certain idea or concept. Likewise, a book can be misused and misread or read lightly for the sake of information only. This is why the main purpose of this book is not only to understand why we need to read, but to read to enhance our understanding further, and to re-learn how to read well.

In 2010, a Pew Research survey of hundreds of prominent thinkers was conducted. Almost 80% of them agreed that by 2020, human intelligence would be enhanced because of the unprecedented access to the information we now have on the internet. Fast forward to today, it can be seen that we didn't get any smarter nor are we making better choices [3]. So what happened? And most importantly, how can reading help us enhance our intelligence?

Making Better Choices

Let us first examine what human intelligence is to try and understand how the plethora of information we now have access to did not enhance intelligence. By definition, human intelligence is our mental ability to reason, solve problems, and learn. It integrates several cognitive functions including our perception, memory, attention, and language [4]. Obviously, such cognitive functions, or at least one of them, need to be improved to enhance human intelligence further.

So what happened during this decade when almost most humans had online access? Many studies have been conducted about the negative effects of the Internet throughout this past decade. First, using the Internet has, in fact, reduced our short-term memory because our brains are learning that we do not need to remember anything. We can, at any time, access the information and google anything we want, so there is no need for us to remember. This phenomenon is dubbed the "Google Effect" [5].

Additionally, the Internet, being highly condensed with information and stimuli, has given rise to "cursory reading, hurried and distracted thinking, and superficial learning" [6]. So technically, plenty of our cognitive functions are decreasing with extensive Internet usage. However, one cannot ignore the importance of the Internet, which does, in fact, contain everything humans have known, nor can we disregard its necessity in our daily lives. So how can we make better choices and ultimately enhance human intelligence to counter such effects on our cognitions?

The Basis Of Our Evolution

For centuries, and for as long as writing has existed, reading has helped us pass along information from one generation to the next. It would have been practically impossible to make any advance in science, medicine, or any other field if it wasn't for reading.

By reading what has been discovered earlier, we can continue to evolve. When someone writes down what they discovered, and everyone else can read it, someone out there will add to it. And the circle continues and still does up until now. With reading, we have managed to evolve as a species.

We have already mentioned the two different kinds of thinking. Whoever contributed to our evolution as humans in any field definitely had analytical thinking. They saw a problem and worked towards solving it. However, there is no new knowledge; everything anyone has come up with was at least partly based on previous knowledge. This is why any research conducted and deemed trustworthy begins with a literature review section. Reviewing past literature about the subject of any problem one is trying to solve is the backbone of any research. It is the anchor onto which new ideas are attached [7].

So our evolution as humans needed, and still does need, analytic thinkers who read. So technically, contemplative thinking is a prerequisite to analytical thinking. If we want to make good use of a powerful tool like the Internet, which provides us with the means to think analytically, we first need to step back and learn to think contemplatively. And our minds can be trained to do so by reading books.

Weigh And Consider

No one is born with an opinion, but as we grow up, we start forming our ideas and thoughts. As we become more conscious about the world around us, we start to learn more about our own interests and form our own opinions. This is what allows us to make choices and decisions, and this is what actually requires analytical thinking. But how do we make up our minds about things? How do we form our opinions in the first place?

This is where reading comes in. So why read? We read to strengthen ourselves and to fortify those interests we are discovering about ourselves. We read to create the "literature review" of our life experiences and thoughts. As social species, we read what others have thought and experienced, what others have discovered, and what conclusions others have drawn, forming an opinion of our own. And just like Sir Francis Bacon once wrote, we read "to weigh and consider" [8].

To weigh and consider what is being read, we need to read contemplatively. This leads us to actually gain the information - and not just access it - which ultimately helps us form our opinions. And this is when analytical thinking should start, with the information we have gained as the means to solve an issue.

If we think back to the cognitive functions of human intelligence, we find that all can be improved easily by reading. First, our language definitely gets better with the more reading we do. When reading contemplatively, our attention and concentration increase, which can in turn help with our memory functions. And last but not least, our whole perception can change and be enhanced when coming face-to-face with new ideas to think about, consider, and contemplate.

Separate The Wheat From The Chaff

Many things on the Internet are useless - just like many books aren't really worth reading. Another skill we need to read better is critical thinking. It will help us choose what we read. The American Philosophical Association has come to a consensus about the portrait of "the ideal critical thinker" as someone who is [9]:

- Inquisitive in nature
- Well-informed
- Trustful of reason
- Open-minded
- Flexible
- Fair-minded in evaluation
- Honest in facing personal biases
- Prudent in making judgments

- Willing to reconsider
- Clear about issues
- Orderly in complex matters
- Diligent in seeking relevant information
- Reasonable in the selection of criteria
- Focused on inquiry
- Persistent in seeking results

As someone who is willing to learn to read better, make better choices, and further enhance their intelligence, we need to check off every criterion on this list. Critical thinking is needed in every aspect of life, and not just reading. It helps us make better choices in both our personal and professional lives.

But how can we use those skills off of this checklist to make better choices? How can we better choose what we read, whether online or off a bookshelf? If knowledge is simply a set of information, then we can take everything we read at face value. But in fact, knowledge also entails the interpretation of this information.

A critical reader rarely questions the facts but assesses the quality of what is written by interpreting how they are stated. They interpret whether there is enough evidence to support a claim that is made, whether there is another possible interpretation that wasn't considered, and whether the author has taken into consideration how their interpretation applies to other cases [10].

In order to choose better what to read, there are several principles we should consider [11]:

- The credibility of the person or source
- The circumstance or context in which the claim is made
- The justification made in support of that claim
- The nature of the claim itself
- The corroboration from other sources

Whatever we encounter, whatever book or article we wish to read, we usually consider if we like it or not based on our taste, which is totally feasible. But we also need to consider those five principles and make a critical judgment of whether it is worthy of our time or not in the first place.

Action Steps

Taking into consideration the five principles of critical reading, read through the two articles suggested below and try to make a critical choice of which one would be more beneficial for you to read. Both Articles tackle a similar main topic.

Article A -

Bloomberg hits the jackpot: NYC students can't read, write, or do arithmetic[12]

Article B -

How New York City Is Working to Improve Students' Social-Emotional Learning[13]

After going over the articles, try to answer the below questions:

1. Which article is worthy of your time to read and why?
2. How did you come up with the conclusion?
3. Identify instances where you felt one of the articles isn't convincing you with the claims it is making.
4. Which information have you taken from the articles do you deem as trustworthy? Why?

Summary

Reading books still matters, and many of us, just like Mary, believe so. Yet we first need to understand why it does in our digital world. Reading books helps us think differently, and when we read contemplatively to understand, we gain insight, understand more, and ultimately enhance our intelligence.

The Internet has given us unprecedented access to information at all times, yet hasn't helped enhance our intelligence. This is because gaining knowledge isn't about having access to information. It is about being able to filter through the information, think about it contemplatively in the context in which it is presented, and think about it critically before taking everything we see and read at face value.

Now that we know why reading is necessary in the digital world and the importance of thinking critically in making our choices, many questions remain. How can we read contemplatively? And how can we read better to ultimately enhance our human intelligence? This is what the book is about: learning to read better, understand better, and think better about what we read.

Key Takeaways

- There are two kinds of thinking: Analytical thinking and contemplative thinking.
- Analytical thinking is transitive and goal-oriented, in which information is used as a means to reach an explanation.
- Contemplative thinking is intransitive and experiential, in which reflection is the end goal. Information, in this case, is worthless without its context.
- Critical thinking is a crucial aspect for humans to make better choices, and we need to be critical when choosing what we read.
- Gaining knowledge isn't only about accessing information; it is about evaluating it critically.

2

READING FOR INSIGHT

HOW YOUR READING APPROACH AFFECTS HOW
YOU RETAIN INFORMATION

The Desire To Learn

As a fresh graduate, Ryan is looking forward to launching his career. He is in the process of applying for internships and is temporarily working at a coffee shop to pay the bills. With the world becoming increasingly dependent on online presence, he feels it is of the utmost importance to educate himself about online marketing.

So he buys a few books about the subject matter and tries to delve deeper into the tools, methodologies, and strategies of online marketing. He picks up one of the books every night to read a few pages. He understands what he is reading and goes to sleep feeling a little more illuminated about online marketing.

The next morning while he is at work, he tries to recall what he read, but everything seems fuzzy to him. "Let me just concentrate on work now. There are so many distractions around me," he thinks and continues with his day.

He meets up with his friends later that night and shares with them excitedly that he is learning about online marketing, a much-needed skill in today's business world. When he tries to explain further what he has learned, he stumbles while trying to utter a comprehensible sentence. He then gives up and changes the subject in desperation. He goes back home feeling depressed and thinks that he needs to concentrate more and read more, in hopes of being able to master the topic.

Passive Reading

What Ryan is going through isn't too uncommon for readers. His excitement has led him to go through the books as quickly as possible and to gain knowledge within, as soon as he can. A common flaw that all excited knowledge seekers tend to exhibit. This often leaves them unable to grasp the new information as well as they initially intend to.

Reading isn't truly just about reading the words, and it isn't only about understanding their individual meanings. As you are reading this sentence, you can understand every word as a literate adult. But reading a paragraph, a chapter, or a complete book, needs much more than understanding the words.

Sometimes you find yourself reading and re-reading a paragraph or a chapter, but not being able to truly grasp the essence of what it says. And this is because you are reading passively, someone who, just like Ryan, is driven by his excitement to master a new subject. So he goes over some words on a few pages and expects himself to fully grasp all of the info. His inability to do so has nothing to do with his intelligence or apprehension skills. But it has everything to do with *how* he is reading the book.

In 2001, Dr. William Perry, a Harvard educational psychologist, conducted an experiment on what he has dubbed as "obedient purposelessness" in reading. He assigned a chapter in a book for students to read and told them that they needed to write an essay about what they've learned in about 20 minutes. Only 15 out of 1500 students were able to write a short statement about the basic theme of the chapter [1]. Our habit of passive reading stems from how we always used to read for the sake of successfully making it through to the next grade. This leads us to have no control over what we understand and what we remember [2].

Features Of Passive Reading

Let us first be clear about the terminology. It is practically impossible to be a completely "passive" reader in the sense that one can't read with immobilized eyes and an asleep mind [3]. But most readers are considered to be passive. And this is because of the habit we gained as students. We've all been inclined to skim through a text to gain the least amount of information needed to pass an upcoming test [4].

There is a big difference between reading with questions in mind and reading just for the sake of reading and finishing the book you have on hand. Let us first start by identifying the features of passive reading, and they include [5]:

"Obedient purposelessness" – reading a book without a specific purpose in mind isn't only an inefficient reading practice, but it tends to become boring.

Uncritical reading – reading without questions in mind and blindly considering the author as an authority.

"Finish reading" mentality – having a book on hand and reading it from beginning to end, which would simply give you a sense of achievement.

Unengaged reading – the practice of reading without assessing the weaknesses and strengths of what is written.

Little understanding – reading the words, sentences, and chapters, and finishing the book with little to no understanding of the main point.

Shallow impression – you might have a general impression of what the book has to say after reading, but you will have gained no deep understanding of the subject matter.

Are You A Passive Reader?

As you're reading this book, and as you've already read the introduction and the first chapter, ask yourself these questions:

- Did I start reading with a specific purpose in mind?
- Did I start reading with the mentality of just finishing the book?
- Was I engaged in what it had to say?
- What do I have to say about the main idea discussed so far?
- Did I have specific questions in mind while reading? Was I looking for the answers?

When discussing the difference between an active and a passive reader, we need to be aware that reading can rather be "less or more active," and that our purpose as readers is to become more active while reading [6]. Learning to become an active reader isn't a matter of black and white; it is a process. One has to go through the process to become more active while reading.

The Desire To Learn How To Read

A case study in 2010 highlighted the effect of implementing metacognitive reading strategies on five college students; strategies derived from a study in the eighties, originally dedicated to elementary students. The strategies taught included: connecting one's background knowledge to the text, drawing conclusions from the text, being able to summarize a text, and determining the importance of the text [7].

Implementing such simple strategies has helped college students to move from deciphering words on paper to becoming critical readers and engaging their thoughts and ideas with what is being read. And so they have moved from being passive readers to more active readers. If you look back at the different strategies used in the study, they can all be summarized by simple questions one can have in mind while reading:

- What do I already know about the topic?
- What does the book add to my knowledge?
- What is the main point of the book?
- What did I learn after reading the book?

Features Of Active Reading

There are several different features of active reading which include [8]:

Reading with questions in mind – you can only find an answer in what you're reading if you are, in the first place, asking a question.

Questioning the author – an author who took the time to write a book must be respected, but shouldn't always be taken as infallible.

Being intellectually engaged – if you aren't interested and fully engaged in what you are reading, you might as well be reading random words and sentences.

Engaging in critical reading – predict what comes next and compare what you know with what is being said. Try to have a conversation with the author and develop your arguments.

Drawing conclusions – when you can do so, you have reached a deeper understanding of the subject matter.

Every writer has something to say, and this is why they write in the first place. The reader is at the receiving end of what is being conveyed in the written book. But a receiver's ability to comprehend what the writer has to say depends on how much effort they put into the reading process, as well as the different mental skills used while reading [9].

Becoming An Active Reader

The 2010 case study has concluded the urgent need for college students to re-learn how to read. We reach adulthood after going through school and college, which ought to be our primary source of learning instructions. Yet we end up moving forward into the work environment, without the required tools that allow us to continue to learn. And we have to read to add to our knowledge.

The students that learned to apply different metacognitive reading strategies have experienced a difference in how they read. One of the students has noted that he is no longer *just* reading, but he is actively thinking about what he is reading and ultimately understanding it [10].

Action Steps

Let us try a step-by-step exercise to apply the skills of active reading by going over a simple online article.

You are going to read an article with the title "Why a placebo can work - even when you know it's fake." Before reading the article, try to ask a few questions regarding the title and relate them to your background knowledge.

You might start considering what you already know about a placebo; you could wonder how it would work if someone knows it is a placebo. You would imagine the ways this was tested or who might have written this article. Many ideas could come to your mind by reading the title alone. Acknowledge them and say them out loud.

This is the article's subtitle: "A placebo can trigger pain relief and other benefits even when patients are told the pills they are taking lack therapeutically active ingredients." Are there any additional questions you might ask after reading the subtitle?

You now have a pretty good idea of what the article is about. Are you able to predict what it might say?

A very important aspect of active reading is to stop from time to time and think back at your questions. Did any of them get answers? Are there any additional questions you might ask? So it is a good idea to try and take note of your questions until you get used to reading with questions in mind.

When reading the full article, try to pause after each paragraph. Relate what you've read to your previous knowledge, and ask more questions. This is what active reading is all about. Read the article, "Why a placebo can work—even when you know it's fake,"[11] actively.

Summary

While Ryan's enthusiasm to learn about online marketing is a good driving force, it obviously wasn't enough to master the subject. He is excited to say that he knows about online marketing, so he is going through the purchased books as quickly as he can.

This quick reading has led him to read incomprehensibly. He was indeed able to read the words on the pages, but he was unable to talk about the subject confidently. What he lacks is being more active while reading.

However, reading actively doesn't only entail absorbing the information on the pages. It requires understanding new concepts and ideas. In order to understand more, one will need to make use of a few cognitive abilities and critical thinking strategies, which we still need to discuss in detail, to achieve a complete understanding of the concepts.

<u>Key Takeaways</u>

- Reading is much more than understanding the words on the paper.

- A passive reader is like a student trying to read his assigned books to pass the exam.
- An active reader engages with the writer, adds his knowledge to what he is reading, and reads with questions in mind.
- Becoming an active reader is a process that needs constant practice. One needs to engage his mind while reading. As much as you are more active while reading, the better you will understand what you're reading.

3

DON'T JUST READ

WHY CRITICAL READING IS IMPORTANT AND HOW YOU CAN TAKE ADVANTAGE OF THIS SKILL

L aura's brother has been in the hospital for three weeks after contracting COVID-19. She is really worried about him and tries as much as possible to learn everything she can about what is going on with him. She is researching as much as she can about the disease from any credible sources she can find, and she is getting updates from his doctors on his condition as much as possible. However, she keeps having the urge to understand more about what is happening to his body, as he doesn't seem to be getting any better.

Every day, she goes online to try to learn more about the disease that has caused the worldwide pandemic. Before her brother got sick, she listened to the information about COVID-19 generally, understood the symptoms, and knew what needed to be done to avoid contracting the disease. But after her brother got sick and had to be hospitalized, she wanted to learn more about what it exactly does, even though she doesn't have a medical background.

The abundance of information, articles, and news about the disease overwhelms her. She wants to understand but whenever she reads something, she feels she is cramming her mind. Either she doesn't understand enough or is not getting sufficient information from what she reads.

Laura is intelligent. However, no matter how much she tries, she doesn't know how to make the most out of her reading. She isn't able to fully grasp the ideas she reads. So what is Laura doing wrong? And how can she overcome the difficulties of reading?

Defining The Goals Of Reading

Before tackling in depth the issue that Laura is facing, we first should distinguish between the different goals of reading when we choose something to read. The first goal can be for mere entertainment, which is perfectly plausible to do. In fact, we should read for pleasure, as this would help us to love reading [1]. Additionally, reading for pleasure has been proven to have many benefits that include but aren't restricted to: "reading attainment and writing ability," "a better understanding of other cultures," and "a greater insight into human nature and decision-making" [2].

The second goal of reading is to gain information. Regardless of the topic we are looking into, we read to increase our information bank. We read the news to know what is going on around us, and we read history, for instance, to gain more knowledge about what happened before our time. And the third goal is to understand. The difference between the last two goals of reading lies in the various experiences your mind goes through while reading. It is worth noting, however, that it is not always easy to distinguish between reading for information and reading for understanding.

We will focus on this difference in order to define and make use of the different mechanics of decoding and comprehending the messages in a book. The reason we will not be concentrating on the first goal – reading for pleasure – is because there are no specific cognitive abilities required to read purely for entertainment. In fact, reading for pleasure "requires the least amount of effort" and has no rules to abide by [3].

Making The Distinction

There is a fine line between reading for the sake of information and reading for understanding, and it is crucial to understand the difference. When reading a book, or anything else for that matter, two different scenarios occur in the relationship between your mind and the text in front of you [4]:

1. You understand what it says and what you read is perfectly intelligible to you in terms of the information it contains.

2. You understand that you aren't understanding enough

and might need to refer to another source or another person to understand what it says.

The second scenario is what Laura is facing. To clearly exemplify this difference, let us take two snippets from articles that Laura has read about COVID-19.

Top health officials are warning that one-third of U.S. residents live in areas where the COVID-19 threat is so high people should "consider" masking up in indoor spaces.

The seven-day average for COVID-19 hospital admissions rose 19% from last week, according to the director of the Centers for Disease Control and Prevention.

Meanwhile, an analysis found that COVID-19 vaccines could have saved 319,000 American lives, had the individuals received the doses. Researchers created a dashboard that displayed vaccine-preventable deaths per 1 million residents for every U.S. state and the country overall. The dashboard also shows an "alternative scenario" depicting what the number of deaths would've been if 85%, 90% or 100% of adults received vaccines.

Snippet 1

The effect of lymphopenia on microbial infection

Lymphopenia is a common feature in patients with COVID-19 and may be a critical factor associated with disease severity and mortality.[21] There is a crosstalk between immune homeostasis and microbe in several diseases.[56] (1,3)-β-D-glucan, a well-known polysaccharide, is a key structural component of the fungal cell wall. In our previous study, we found that in patients with severe COVID-19 and low lymphocyte levels, (1,3)-β-D-glucan levels are significantly higher than in patients with high lymphocyte levels.[27] Moreover, most patients infected with microbe had low lymphocyte levels, indicating that patients with lymphopenia are more prone to microbial infection.[27] Chen et al.[3] demonstrated that multiple microbes could be cultured from one patient, which is similar to our study findings. Overall, the findings indicate that microbial infection in patients with COVID-19 promotes disease progression and severity.

By reading snippet 1 [5], almost every literate adult can understand what the article is talking about. The reader is aware of what COVID-19 is, what "masking up" refers to, and what the COVID-19 vaccines are. Everything in that article expresses a common understanding that we have before encountering this article. It has given us additional information about new statistics about the subject matter, but it hasn't truly added anything to our general understanding of the topic.

The text in snippet 2 [6], on the other hand, might be a little more complex. Unless you happen to be familiar with the medical terms, you read the English words and realize that you do not understand what it says. In order to fully grasp it, you will either need to refer to someone or another book that would help in explaining it.

To understand better what we read, we want to focus on the third goal of reading, and that is to read for understanding. This can be accomplished by the power of the reader's mind alone without the need for external help. This would allow you to lift yourself "from a state of understanding less to one of understanding more" [7].

When To Read For Understanding

Before discussing how we can achieve more understanding while reading, we need to be aware of when we will need this skill. Two conditions should be present when such reading takes place [8]:

ONE - There should be an "initial inequality in understanding." This means that the writer must know more about the topic than you do.

TWO - You need to aim to "overcome this inequality" while reading. As long as you are reading and understanding more about the topic, this inequality gap narrows.

So going back to the previous examples of the texts that Laura has chosen to read, we can see that in snippet 1, the writer conveys information that we might not be aware of but has nothing to teach us that would enhance our understanding of the topic. However, in snippet 2, there are new concepts and the writer is more knowledgeable in terms of medical details about COVID-19.

In this chapter, we aim to increase our understanding of a text such as the one in snippet 2. If we learn to do that, then reading for information (like reading snippet 1) becomes an easy task.

Critical Reading

We have touched upon the importance of being critical while choosing what to read in chapter 1. The critical choice we make will be the basis of the first condition of reading for understanding. By critically considering the book, we will be able to see if there is indeed a margin of inequality between the writer and me. By evaluating the writer, we will determine if they have the upper hand and can teach us something with their book. Therefore, we can decide whether or not the book is worthy of reading for understanding.

Once this is done, we will need to work on completing the second condition of understanding more, which is trying to narrow the gap of inequality between the reader and the writer. That is to learn the process of understanding more.

Laura is an active reader, but currently lacks the capacity to make use of her critical thinking while reading. She does read with questions in mind, as she is actively trying to find answers about the disease, but she also needs to adopt a "more detailed approach to critical reading" [9].

Five Critical Questions

When you are face-to-face with a text and can read it actively, you should also read it critically. This will set you on the path of understanding more about what it says. The following five basic critical questions will help in undertaking a detailed analysis of the text [10].

1. *Why am I reading this?*

This question will offer you a way to focus on what you want out of what you are reading rather than blindly following the author's agenda. Every author has an opinion, and regardless of how well they try to remain objective, it is not always the case. This question will help you to focus on your needs instead of what the author wants to convey through their writing.

2. *What is the author trying to do?*

There are many different examples of why an author writes something. Some authors aim to report something, criticize someone else's work, develop a theory, express an opinion, or simply want to give advice. Once you know the author's intention, you will be able to relate it to what you want to understand from what you're reading.

3. *What is the author saying that relates to what I want to learn?*

This question covers what the text is about and how it overlaps with both the author's concerns and your interests. With this question in mind, you can discover what the author has to give you in terms of what you are seeking.

4. *How much did the author convince me?*

This question lies at the core of what a critical reader does. Even though you have deemed the book and its author reliable, they might not convince you with their arguments or claims. You will need to look out for any assumptions made by the author.

5. *What use can I make of this?*

How much would you agree or disagree with the author? How will you use the information in this text to further your understanding of the topic? This is where you would draw a conclusion after reading.

Solving The Puzzles In A Text

While reading critically with those questions as a guide, you will sometimes need to approach the text like a puzzle. Actually, reading for the purpose of understanding is much more like studying what the book says than simply reading it.

To increase your understanding of what snippet 2 says, reading from the first sentence to the end will prove to be fruitless – unless you are familiar with the medical jargon used. When reading to increase your understanding, you should go back and forth, highlight and underline, take notes, draw diagrams, and, most importantly, take some breaks to think and consider what has been read [11].

Let us go back to snippet 2 and try to solve the puzzle of what the text has to say. If you follow the notes from 1 to 3 in the below figure, you will see how to deal with the text to simplify what it says. In this manner, you can understand more simply by using your mind. Texts like these tax our brains. Nevertheless, with such an activity, you'd be stretching yourself; you achieve this elevation with the assistance of the author who had something to teach you [12].

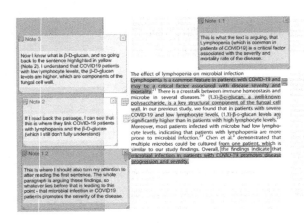

Note 3
Now I know what is β-D-glucan, and so going back to the sentence highlighted in yellow (Note 2). I understand that COVID19 patients with low lymphocyte levels, the β-D-glucan levels are higher, which are components of the fungal cell wall.

Note 2
If I read back the passage, I can see that this is where they link COVID-19 patients with lymphopenia and the β-D-glucan (which I still don't fully understand)

Note 1.2
This is where I should also turn my attention to after reading the first sentence. The whole paragraph is arguing those findings, so whatever lies before that is leading to this point - that microbial infection in COVID19 patients promotes the severity of the disease.

Note 1.1
This is what the text is arguing, that Lymphopenia (which is common in patients of COVID19) is a critical factor associated with the severity and mortality rate of the disease.

The effect of lymphopenia on microbial infection
Lymphopenia is a common feature in patients with COVID-19 and may be a critical factor associated with disease severity and mortality.[16] There is a crosstalk between immune homeostasis and microbe in several diseases.[16] (1,3)-β-D-glucan, a well-known polysaccharide, is a key structural component of the fungal cell wall. In our previous study, we found that in patients with severe COVID-19 and low lymphocyte levels, (1,3)-β-ᴅ-glucan levels are significantly higher than in patients with high lymphocyte levels.[27] Moreover, most patients infected with microbe had low lymphocyte levels, indicating that patients with lymphopenia are more prone to microbial infection.[27] Chen et al.[3] demonstrated that multiple microbes could be cultured from one patient, which is similar to our study findings. Overall, the findings indicate that microbial infection in patients with COVID-19 promotes disease progression and severity.

Taking Control Of Your Reading Process

Using your cognitive abilities in the reading process is another essential cognitive skill. You will need to be fully aware of what you are reading and take control of the process. Several steps help you achieve this, and you will notice how those steps intersect with being an active reader and with critical thinking processes [13]:

1. *Predict* what the book or text is about. This can be done while reading. You can make a prediction about an idea you believe the book might follow or a conclusion that the writer is going to arrive at. As you read on, your predictions are either confirmed or denied. In the latter's case, you'd have to make new predictions and keep on going.

2. *Picture* the ideas as you read on. Form mental images of the concepts, or try to envision the action in your mind.

Any visual conception of what you're reading will help increase your understanding.

3. *Relate* to your previous knowledge and make comparisons with what you know or what you have once experienced. This will help to make it easier to understand what you are reading.

4. *Monitor* your comprehension of every part. You will notice whenever you read a passage and feel that you haven't fully grasped the idea. Do not ignore this feeling and continue reading without trying to understand it. If you fail to understand it, you will need to try reading it differently, as we have done in the previous example.

5. *Correct* any gaps you might have in your understanding. Sometimes you might feel the need to go back in order to understand an idea, or even read further. Identify the gaps as you monitor your comprehension, and seek a resolution, whether by going backward or forward.

Action Steps

Let us try to read other parts of the COVID-19 article that Laura attempted to read. Head over to the article "COVID-19: immunopathogenesis and Immunotherapeutics" (https://www.nature.com/articles/s41392-020-00243-2#citeas)[14] and choose to read a few paragraphs.

Make use of the tools to read the article critically, try to understand them, and narrow the gap between you and the author.

Here is a suggestion for a paragraph to decipher and understand: "Comparison with SARS-CoV-induced immunopathology."

Summary

Do not just read, but also aim to understand more. Aim to leave that book or the text you have more enlightened, with additional gained knowledge and not just mere information. To achieve this goal successfully, you will need to use several cognitive abilities. You will understand more about any given topic by using your mind solely, as long as you use the necessary abilities.

Laura can only achieve her goal of increasing her knowledge of COVID-19 and its impact by following several steps. She needs to critically read the text she has, decipher it like a puzzle by going back and forth, and take control of her reading process. Ultimately, she finishes her articles more enlightened about the topic.

However, when her mother asks her about her brother's condition, she finds it hard to explain the newly acquired information. She understands what she has read, but she is unable to explain it. So what is she missing?

Key Takeaways

- The three goals of reading are reading for pleasure, reading for information, and reading for understanding, where our focus in this book lies.
- Critical thinking helps in choosing what we read, while critical reading allows us to understand more of what we read to gain knowledge from what we want to learn.
- Reading to understand more can be achieved by approaching it more like studying. We should try to decipher the text by going back and forth, taking notes, summarizing, and making conclusions.
- To understand more when we read, we should take control of the process.

4

READ TO DISCOVER

WHAT IS THE DIFFERENCE BETWEEN LEARNING BY INSTRUCTION AND LEARNING BY DISCOVERY? AND WHY SHOULD I KNOW IT?

Jim was always a poor student in school. In high school, he kept skipping classes and failed his sophomore year. He was never interested in studying or in anything school-related. He dropped out and became a construction worker. He loved working with his hands and grew to love the job. Jim excelled at his work and became a supervisor. He married a lovely woman and has a daughter who just turned 14 years old.

As his little girl grew, he began to worry that they'd grow apart. Now that she's 14, he finds they have little in common and can't find topics that interest her to talk to her about. When he heard that her school was organizing a father-daughter book club, he was excited to take part just to be closer to his daughter. However, he realized later that he had to read books to be part of the club.

He hasn't held a book for a long time and really wasn't looking forward to doing so. However, when he saw his little girl excited about the book club, he decided to go for it anyway just to have something to talk about and spend time together. The first book they had to read was Harper Lee's *To Kill a Mockingbird*.

At first, it was a real burden and a headache to pick up that book and read. However, he enjoyed how his daughter started challenging him on who will finish this or that chapter first. He also loved the time they spent discussing the story. So he kept opening that book and reading it every night. When they met at the book club, he was outspoken and excited to share his ideas about the book. He was very surprised, and he even told his wife, "I don't know what my high school pals would say if they see me now being part of a book club! I despised reading. But you know, I am really enjoying this. And I have no idea why!"

Jim has had two different experiences with reading books. The first one was back in high school, an experience that he so despised that he dropped out. The second experience is at the book club with his daughter, which he found himself enjoying. He started looking forward to his reading time and was excited to discuss what he has read. So what is the difference between those two experiences with reading books? And why did he enjoy the second one so much?

Those two experiences show the difference between two

types of learning which will be at the core of this chapter's discussion.

Seeking Enlightenment

When we all had to learn the multiplication table, the teacher simply informed us that, for instance, $3 \times 7 = 21$. We just knew that if we multiply 7 by 3 or 3 by 7, the answer is 21. We had to memorize the multiplication table and tried to give the answers to multiplication problems by exercising our memories. This was part of our learning process. The teacher told us the facts, and we had to keep them in mind. This is how we grew up gaining more information and learning everything throughout school.

However, alternatively, we can understand *why* we get 21 when we multiply 3 by 7 or 7 by 3. Let us try to emulate the process of understanding it. Let's say that I have a basket full of apples. I take three apples at a time and put them in a box. I end up having seven boxes in total. So now, I have 7 boxes, and each one has 3 apples. I can add the numbers of apples in each box, for all 7 boxes. So $3 + 3 + 3 + 3 + 3 + 3 + 3$, which add up to 21. And since I have the same number of apples in each box, I can use multiplication instead of addition. So multiplying the number of apples in each box by the number of boxes gives me $3 \times 7 = 21$.

Similarly, if I put seven apples in each box, I will end up with three boxes. So the total number of apples is $7 + 7 +$

7, which also adds up to 21. And this is why 7 x 3 is also equal to 21.

Understanding The Information

The teacher informs us by saying 3 x 7 = 21. It is an effective learning technique as we are given mathematical facts, but we don't gain anything from it besides information if we simply recall it through our memory.

However, when we understand the operation and how multiplication is connected to addition, we become enlightened. When you are enlightened about something, you can explain it. You know what the teacher or author said, what they meant, and why it is so.

It is worth noting that understanding something cannot occur without getting the information first. Therefore, being informed is, in fact, a prerequisite to understanding, or in other words, being enlightened. This is because you must remember what was said if you want to understand what it means. The important point is not to stop at simply receiving the information [1].

When you read a book, you aim to comprehend its information. While reading for comprehension, you need to think of the words you're reading and the information you are learning. As a reader, when you attempt to construct meaning from the book in front of you, you are building a store of knowledge; and along with that knowledge should come understanding [2].

Types Of Learning

The difference between acquiring knowledge and aiming at understanding what we are reading comes from what Michel de Montaigne, a French Renaissance philosopher, calls "a doctoral ignorance." This ignorance is typical of those who have read many books without understanding what they read. There is, in fact, a very big distinction between reading a lot and reading well. And to understand this difference, we need to distinguish between two types of learning: by instruction and by discovery [3].

Instruction Vs. Discovery

When we were at school, instructive learning was dominant. The teacher stood in front of the class, either telling us information or asking us to read that information from a book. This is learning by instruction. However, discovery is another way of gaining knowledge. When you learn by discovery, you are able to explain the information you have acquired and not just recall the information. When you research a topic, dig deeper and investigate it, or even merely reflect on the information without having someone teaching you about it, you are learning by discovery.

Both types of learning have their benefits. If we take learning by instruction first, it is beneficial to learn using this method if one lacks prior knowledge about the topic. This is why this type of learning is mostly used in schools. It is helpful when the students need guidance to understand the topic well. Nevertheless, as good and beneficial as it is for students, it has many drawbacks.

Having spent most of our lives learning by instruction, we end up facing many difficulties in the business world. In a typical classroom, the teacher lays out the information for students and then gives problems for them to solve using that information. However, as adults, we first face the problem, then we seek solutions to those problems. So learning by instruction would be useless to us at this point.

In contrast, when we learn by discovery, we actually learn core concepts that will help us deal with real-life problems. Our learning process in the real world occurs in the journey of solving the problem by researching, investigating, and then discovering the different paths toward finding the solution. Ultimately, learning by discovery gives us the necessary thinking skills to help us to retain knowledge. Those skills are divided into the following three main phases [4]:

1. Understanding the context – we are confronted with a problem that allows us to get familiar with a topic.

2. Exploring and analyzing – the research phase in which we tend to collect as much information as possible about the topic and try to analyze the details of the problem. Along the way, we gain information which we will need to answer the problem.

3. Drawing conclusions – once we have gained new insights and have refined our understanding of the

problem on hand, we can then interpret it and attempt to solve it.

Active Learning And Active Reading

It should be noted that learning by instruction is by no means a passive action. As reading is never completely passive, learning cannot be inactive. This is why learning by instruction can also be called "aided discovery." As an active action, learning by instruction or by aided discovery entails thinking during the learning process.

However, when we learn by discovery, we will need to put in more effort to understand. This is because thinking comprises only one part of the learning process. We should use our senses and our imaginations, by observing, remembering, and constructing abstract notions that can't be observed [5]. We can do this by practicing and refining our critical thinking. In fact, this crucial mental skill actually starts with active learning [6].

When you learn by instruction with a teacher's assistance, you will not be incorporating all of your mental faculties in the learning process. This only helps you acquire information. In contrast, when learning without a teacher, which is learning by discovery, you not only need to think about what you are learning, but you also have to make use of everything you have to actually understand. This is active learning, and it can only be achieved with a deeper understanding and a flexible way of thinking [7].

Active reading includes all the same skills involved in learning by discovery. One needs to be observant, have a readily available memory, use imagination, and have the intellectual ability to analyze and reflect [8]. When we read to understand and not just to get information, we go beyond the mere information in the book or the literal meaning of a text. Active reading is like active learning in that we have a deeper understanding of what we are reading, develop insight, and think critically and more deeply. When we read, we question, interpret, and evaluate [9].

Just as a scientist learns about any new concept by observing the world, questioning, analyzing, and concluding, a reader should do the same. The book is the world you are about to discover, and when you start questioning, it provides the answers as long as you think and analyze [10].

The Sophistication Of Thought

When we want to learn actively through reading, we need to treat reading as a learning method. Three main levels of comprehension are needed to successfully achieve learning by discovery through a book or text. Those levels are hierarchal in terms of the sophistication required in our thought process [11]. Within each one of those levels, the reader can generate a series of questions from the text using the QAR technique, which stands for *Question, Answer, and Relationships* [12]. By going through each level and asking all of the questions, the reader learns by discovering the text.

Level One – Literal

The first level of reading is a literal one. That is to read exactly what is in the text as it is presented. This is where the reader can identify the main idea, is able to recall the details that support it, and organize the main points in chronological order [13]. The main questions that the reader asks throughout this level have explicitly stated answers within the text [14]. Such questions include *who, what, when, and where* [15]?

Level Two – Interpretive

The second level of reading is the interpretive one. This is when we read between the lines. We read to understand what is implied within the text [16]. The reader at this level of comprehension can anticipate a consequence, generalize, and identify reasons [17]. When a reader is interpreting a text, they would be thinking and searching for in-text connections [18]. The reader can ask questions such as *how, why, and what if* [19]?

Level Three - Applied

The third level is when we read "beyond the lines" [20]. This is when reading becomes learning by discovery. The reader would take what is said in the text (level one), and what can be inferred by what's in the text (level two) and apply the ideas beyond that text [21]. At this level, the questions asked should be motivated by the text, but the answers would be generated from the reader's prior knowledge [22]. So, the reader uses their knowledge and experiences to create answers to the questions. The questions asked are usually open-ended, allowing the reader to generalize, compare, judge, recommend, suggest, decide, and even create alternative solutions or endings [23].

Action Steps

To achieve learning by discovery, aka without assistance, the active reader needs to apply four main skills that we mentioned in this chapter and they are:

- Being observant
- Having a readily available memory
- Using the imagination
- Analyzing and reflecting

By keeping those skills in mind and applying the three levels of comprehension, take the time to read the short story by F. Scott Fitzgerald entitled *Winter Dreams*[24].

If you haven't come across any of Fitzgerald's writing before, you must know that the American writer's style requires you to apply all of those skills in order to fully grasp the story he is telling and the moral behind it. Fitzgerald extensively used symbolism and imagery to convey ideas while simultaneously evoking feelings and moods [25]. One will ultimately really benefit from reading, understanding, and interpreting Fitzgerald's stories.

After thoroughly going over the tale, try to answer the following questions:

1. How does Dexter's social status change and why?

2. Why doesn't Dexter marry neither Judy nor Irene?

3. Fitzgerald's style is infused with imagery that mixes the character's fiction with reality. Find a few examples of imagery that perfectly convey the complexity of Dexter and Judy's relationship. How is this achieved?

4. What did Dexter lose at the end? Which human condition is conveyed in this loss?

5. Can you connect Dexter's story with the American Dream?

Summary

There are different experiences that you can go through when reading a book. And Jim has had two different ones, one that he despised and the other he ended up enjoying extremely. When you take a book and decide to discover what it has to say, you will find joy in that discovery. You will learn without a tutor telling you what to look for, and you might draw your own conclusions.

Jim had no interest in books until he found out that the words within the page could make you explore the world within that book with the sole power of your mind. What he must have disliked about his high school experience with books were the limits that the teachers and the curriculum set. With the book club, he enjoyed being the tutor and student, asking and answering, searching and analyzing, and getting to understand and learning by discovering.

In the chapters so far, we went over how a reader can read actively. We also realized how the goal of reading can help in determining the way we read. And we now know that as much effort one puts into reading, the better we read. In this chapter, we differentiated between instruction-based and discovery-based reading. All such tools are helpful to help us read better, and if we manage to implement them properly, we will read better. However, we still lack the essential skills that help us move from one level of reading to the next.

Key Takeaways

- There are two types of learning: Learning by instruction and learning by discovery.
- Learning by instruction is when someone lays out the information for you, and you recall it by remembering what you learned.
- Learning by discovery is when you accomplish learning without assistance. Thinking skills are required to successfully achieve this:

1. Understanding the context
2. Exploring and analyzing
3. Drawing conclusions

- Learning by discovery can be accomplished by active reading with the use of four main skills that are required to understand the text:

1. Being observant of the information
2. Making use of your memory
3. Using your imagination
4. Analyzing and reflecting

- When reading a text, there are three levels of comprehension. At each level, the reader asks different questions to successfully learn and understand what is written:

1. Literal level - reading exactly what is written.
2. Interpretive level – reading what is implied.
3. Applied level – analyzing the information and applying it outside the boundaries of the text.

5

FROM BASICS TO EXPERTISE

HOW YOU CAN GET BEYOND THE SURFACE OF A TEXT AND UNLOCK ITS TRUE POWER

Four Siblings

Audrey, Adam, Jane, and Jack are four successful siblings. Each one works in a different field, but all of them deal with reading for different purposes and in different ways. Audrey is a teacher that teaches young children how to read. Adam is a medical student who has just gotten his fellowship. Jane is a psychologist, and Jack is a Ph.D. student.

Each of the four siblings deals with reading on a different level. Audrey deals with the most basic reading skills with her students. Adam needs to read constantly, but doesn't have the time to read thoroughly every book or research paper that he comes across because of his busy schedule. So he is a fast reader, one that is able to grasp the information quickly. And only when he finds a really important book that he needs, he would then take the time to go through it in detail.

Jane is a practicing psychologist, and in many instances, she encounters a patient whose symptoms she would need to learn more about. So she picks up a psychology book and thoroughly reads it and immerses herself in the details. Jack is completing his dissertation and needs to read many books simultaneously to develop his thesis and complete his research.

All four siblings read, but every one of them reads differently. Those four siblings, and the way they read (or teach reading in the case of Audrey), symbolize the difference between the four levels of reading. Those levels are at the core of this chapter and ultimately, the whole book.

Four Levels Of Reading

Our main purpose in this book is to learn how to read better. And to do anything better, we need to level up. And to be able to level up, we need first to understand each level, how we can proceed, and what is required to step up from one level to another. And this is why, in this chapter, we are going to tackle each widely recognized level of reading in detail [1]. We will explain what each level is all about, its rules, and how we can accomplish reading at that specific level.

Audrey teaches little children how to read. She teaches them what the shapes on the paper refer to, and how they can translate those shapes into words, and words into meaning with only the power of the mind. This is the fundamental level of reading, and we have all gone through this level successfully, or else we wouldn't have been reading or writing this book. This level is also called the "elementary level" and to successfully master it, one learns the basic skills required to read, and receives the most basic reading training.

As a med student, Adam is an excellent reader, who not only knows how to read, but also reads quickly. He is also a critical reader, who knows how to quickly go over books and choose the ones he thinks are worthy of his precious time. This reading level, or pre-reading, is called the "inspectional level." It is used to get the most out of a given book in a short time, a time that is not enough to get everything that you can get out of that book. This level of reading is a perfect solution for someone like Adam, who doesn't have much time to go through the book in detail, but it allows him to successfully understand enough about that book, given the little time he has.

When Jane needs to understand a new concept in psychology to use it in her diagnosis, she needs to read a book about that concept thoroughly. In contrast to the prior level, this reading takes ample time; it requires full concentration and making use of all of the mental capacities of the reader. This is the third level of reading, which is also called "analytical reading." It is complete, thorough, and ultimately considered good reading; it is the best reading one can do. And this is the ultimate level we hope to achieve by the end of this book.

You might now be wondering, if the analytical reading is the ultimate level, why is there a fourth one? As a Ph.D. student, Jack needs to read analytically not just one book, but several books simultaneously to write his dissertation. So this is why the fourth level of reading is considered comparative reading. It is also called "syntopical reading." It is the most demanding type of reading, even if the books are unsophisticated and relatively easy to read.

Chart A Of The Levels Of Reading

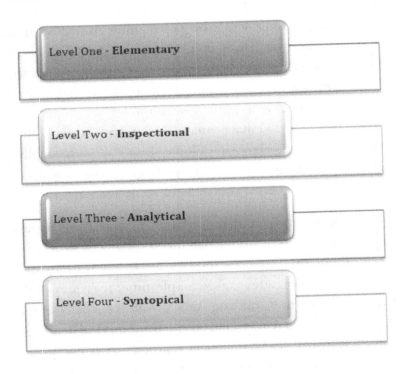

Level One - **Elementary**

Level Two - **Inspectional**

Level Three - **Analytical**

Level Four - **Syntopical**

Level One – Elementary Reading

As mentioned earlier, this is the most basic level of reading. And all literate adults have already mastered this level. The main question a reader asks within this level is, "What does this sentence mean?"

Our main effort at the elementary reading level is to actually be able to identify the words on paper. And once those are identified individually, we can then start to understand the meaning of the sentence as a whole.

Learning How To Read

You are mistaken if you believe that this level is too simple to be included in this book. Reading at this level is actually an astonishing phenomenon if you consider the many components required to master turning simple shapes into meaning [2]. If you've ever tried to learn a second language as an adult, you'd truly understand the magic of reading.

Consider this sentence in Greek for instance:

Ο καιρός γίνεται καλύτερος.

The first level of reading allows you to decipher each letter, word, and entire sentence to understand what it says. And, by the way, it says, "the weather is getting better." Unless you already read Greek, this simple sentence looks incomprehensible to you.

We learned to read as young children, and we weren't aware of the magic it entails. Think of all the phonemes (the units of sounds, how "a" sounds different in words *father* and *snake*); think of the graphemes (when a combination of letters creates a unit sound; the first sound in the word *ghost* created by "g" and "h"), and consider the morphemes that the words contain (with which we can create more complex words; re/appear/ed is one example); think of the propositions, syntactic composition, and stylistics that sentences have [3]. The reader at this level does more than simply understand words, and as literate adults, we do this unconsciously.

At this level of reading, there are four main stages. And every child who learns how to read goes through those stages. On reaching the fourth stage, the child is considered to have a "mature reading ability" [4].

Stage 1 - Reading Readiness

This stage involves preparing and getting the toddler ready to read. The preparation involves different skills that the parents or teachers need to do to make sure that the child is ready to read [5]:

- Physical skills – involves having good visual and auditory perception.
- Intellectual skills – having the necessary amount of visual perception to remember what the letters and words look like.
- Linguistic skills – being able to speak properly and utter complete and correct sentences.

- Personal skills – the child also needs to work well with other students and follow simple directions.

This stage is the first reading level that corresponds to the experiences of children in preschool and kindergarten.

Stage 2 – Reading Simple Materials

At this level, the child connects the shapes of the words with meaning. They are able to learn what the words are by simply looking at the letters. Typically, a child accomplishes this in the first grade.

To be able to read simple materials, the child will have reached mastery of words, and they should already know 300 to 400 words. They usually start reading simple books at this stage and enjoy deciphering what the book says.

Note that research has shown that the reading competence of children at this stage improves, if they are working in pairs within a set of structured activities by the teacher [6]. This is why the personal skills of stage one are crucial for the child's reading readiness.

Stage 3 – Vocabulary Building

As the child learns to read single words, they begin to acquire new vocabulary quickly. At this stage, the child starts to learn different content materials for various purposes, which include science books, social studies, and other languages.

The stage of vocabulary building is reached by the fourth grade. And it is expected that the child starts picking up books and/or magazines to read for their own pleasure. They will also have the ability to read traffic signs, billboards, and even fill out simple forms.

Stage 4 – Refinement Of Reading Skills

The fourth and final stage at the elementary level of reading is "the mature stage of reading." Young teens generally reach this stage and ideally, from then on work on developing their reading skills.

At this level, mature readers can read on their own and are able to compare writing styles and ideas on the same topic. They have the capacity to start thinking critically about books and ideas within the books, but need further work on their skills to become master readers. This is the stage where most readers either remain at the elementary level or start working on going beyond and moving up toward the second level of reading.

This stage is where the learning methods discussed in the previous chapter come into play. The four stages of the elementary reading level are achieved using an instruction-based method. Once the child reaches the fourth stage, they can start using the discovery-based method. This is when a reader starts reading independently and learns by discovering what books can tell them.

The issue is that most students grow into adults yet remain at this first level of reading. Research was conducted on the comprehension calibration among college students, and the researchers noted alarmingly low comprehension calibration correlations. The researchers concluded that there is a need for better reading strategies to help readers improve their comprehension calibration [7]. And this is why we will be detailing the second level of reading that follows the elementary one.

Chart B Of The Levels Of Reading

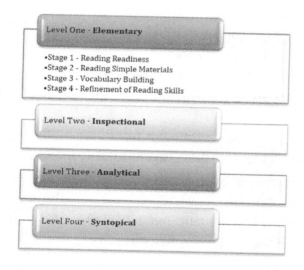

Level Two – Inspectional Reading

By now, we have already mastered the elementary level and are ready to step up. We have touched upon being a critical reader – not just while reading, but also in choosing books to read. This level is key to being a critical reader. However, it does not involve thorough reading of a book.

Adam, the med student, is a master of this level. He needs to thoroughly inspect books and make the most out of them in as little time as possible. This level of reading is "the art of skimming systematically" [8]. It entails examining the book's surface and being able to learn everything that it can teach the reader.

The main questions the reader asks at this level are [9]:

- What type of book is this?
- What is this book about?
- What is the structure of the book?
- What are its parts?

Obviously, a novel is different from a scientific book or a history book. So we first need to identify the kind of book we are reading. We also need to know the topics it discusses, how it is structured, and identify its different parts. This is systematic reading, and it is the first skill used in the second level of reading.

Inspectional reading comprises two different steps that for good readers are actually two different aspects of a single skill. But as we learn to read at this level, we can take each step on its own, and as we become more experienced, we can combine both of them.

Step One - Systematic Skimming

The art of skimming in reading is being able to extract the important parts, including the main points and their relevant substantial details. So technically, skimming is getting the essence of the written material, without having to read it all. It entails skipping parts that you deem are not essential.

This skill helps you with your choice of books. Trying to pick up a book to read critically requires active reading skills. This is how you get to choose if the book deserves a thorough reading, which is the third level of reading. Skimming a book allows us to decide if it deserves an analytic reading or not.

There are several steps to skim a book in as little time as possible, and there are a few things you need to check out [10].

1. *The title page and the preface* – read the title page quickly and the preface if there is one. In this step, you can make note of the subject and the aim of writing the book.

2. *The table of contents* – check the table of contents for a quick look at how the book is structured and what it contains.

3. *The Index* - if included, it will refer you to the exact pages where specific topics and important terms are discussed within the book. You can take a quick look at some of the topics that interest you.

4. *The publisher's blurb* – in many instances, you will find a well-written summary of what the book is about on the back cover. In expository written works, the writer usually helps the publisher to summarize the main points of the book.

At this point, you will have a pretty good idea of whether or not you need to go on reading this book. This is exactly where the critical choice resides. If you decide it is a good book to go through, you can move on to the next steps of skimming.

1. *Most important chapters* – So you decided to move further to read this book, you can identify the most important chapters in the first four steps of skimming. In many instances, depending on the kind of book, you will find opening statements for each chapter. Read those carefully.

2. *Skimming* – Go back and forth turning the pages, read a few paragraphs here or there, and, if necessary, a few pages at a time, but never more.

Step Two – Superficial Reading

Let us say you are face to face with a difficult book to read. Inspectional reading is necessary to help us avoid reading the book in detail and pondering on every word and sentence the first time around. After systematically skimming the book, we should read the book from start to finish without stopping.

This means that there is no need to look at any footnotes, comments, and references within the book. We shouldn't go look up difficult words or even try to understand any details or connotations. If you stop and ponder every word and idea, you will miss the main point and the big picture that the book is trying to convey.

This aspect of the skill needed for inspectional reading requires the reader to have the ability to read quickly. If we want to understand the full picture of a book, we cannot spend several months reading a book. We need to learn how to read swiftly and finish this first superficial reading in as little time as possible.

<u>Improve Your Reading Speed</u>

To improve reading speed, we need to understand the concept behind silent reading. The first thing to be aware of is that reading is a mental activity, and although we look at words with our eyes, reading itself is not done with the eyes.

Your eyes are the means to transport the written words into your brain. And the more words your eyes can take in, the faster you're able to read. So if your eyes transfer a word or two at a time, the reading process is much slower than if they are grabbing a whole line or two. The trick is to try not to read each word, but to let your eyes feed your brain a full sentence or a complete written idea in a single fixation.

To read faster, you need to use your eyes to help your thought process with no interruptions [11]. Consider reading this sentence word by word:

Reading   is   not   done
                with   the   eyes.

The spacing between the words will automatically make it harder for your eyes to fixate on the whole sentence, and you will instantly start reading it word by word. Your brain would be getting each word and waiting for the next to understand the meaning fully. But if you read the entire sentence at once, you will read quickly.

Different Speed Levels
A good reader needs to have the ability to read quickly. However, it must be noted that they should also be able to read at different speed levels and know when to use each. Inspectional reading should be done rather quickly, but this isn't only because we know how to read quickly.

It is mainly because we know when to read quickly, which parts should be read thoroughly, and which parts can be completely skipped. In fact, inspectional reading doesn't entail that the readers read the whole book. It is about varying the approach to reading based on the purposes in mind.

Even in the next level of reading which is definitely much more time-consuming than inspectional reading, the reader needs to be able to read at different speeds. Every book contains parts that we can skim through and other parts that need thorough reading. It comes back to the reader's ability to understand the aim of the book and identify accordingly the important parts that need to be read slowly.

Analytical reading is ordinarily much slower than inspectional reading. Still, even in analytical reading, you should not read all of it at the same rate of speed. Every book, no matter how difficult, contains interstitial material that can be and should be read quickly; and every good book also contains matter that is difficult and should be read very slowly.

Chart C Of The Levels Of Reading

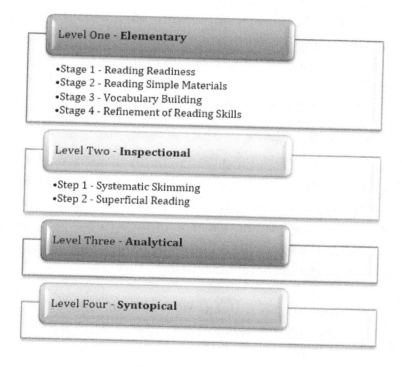

Level One - **Elementary**

- Stage 1 - Reading Readiness
- Stage 2 - Reading Simple Materials
- Stage 3 - Vocabulary Building
- Stage 4 - Refinement of Reading Skills

Level Two - **Inspectional**

- Step 1 - Systematic Skimming
- Step 2 - Superficial Reading

Level Three - **Analytical**

Level Four - **Syntopical**

Level Three – Analytical Reading

This third level of reading is the most sophisticated kind of reading a good reader can do. But analytical reading is barely necessary if your goal as a reader is for mere entertainment or simply to get information. Analytical reading is predominantly used for understanding a book on a deep level.

The core principle of reading at this level comes down to organization: organization of thought, goals of reading, and asking the right questions in an organized way. And there are many questions an analytical reader must ask. An analytical reader is an active reader, and we have already covered a good part of what an active reader needs to do to read actively. However, the core essence of reading at this level is to ask questions while you are reading the book and answer them as you go on reading.

What You Should Ask

Any reading at a level higher than the elementary reading level entails having a habit of asking the correct questions in an organized way and at the right time. And asking those questions is the essence of active reading. An analytical reader must keep in mind four main questions as they read and attempt to find their answers [12]:

- What is the book about? What is the main theme of the book? And how did the author develop it?
- What are the main ideas and arguments that the author used to relay the message?

- Is what this book says true or not?
- What is the significance of the information within this book?

An analytical reader should think about and answer those questions as they are reading and in that same order. It is practically insignificant to ask about the arguments and details of a book (question 2) if one doesn't know what the book is about. Similarly, one cannot make up their mind about a book and decide whether it is true or not (question 3) if one doesn't know all of the details. And if a reader wants to determine the significance of the book (question 4), they need to know what lies between its pages and decide whether it is true in whole or in part.

Those four main questions provide the framework that an analytical reader needs to follow while reading. However, being able to answer them entails a much greater effort than just simply asking a few questions. And knowing what those questions are is not enough to read analytically. You must build up the habit of asking them while reading, and you must also learn how to answer them accurately.

To successfully answer the questions, an analytical reader needs to go through three stages while reading a book at this level. First, we need to know what the book is about and how it is structured. Second, we need to understand the content of the book. Third, we need to know how to criticize the book. Each stage has a set of rules that one must follow to fully answer the questions above [13].

Stage One – A Book's Structure

Rule 1 – Identify the kind of book

After an inspectional reading of a book, you should know what kind of book it is. And that involves reviewing the title, preface, and table of contents, amongst other clues to identify which category this book falls into.

There are many kinds of books out there, and the first thing one needs to do is identify what kind it is. Is it non-fiction, a novel, or a play? Is it a scientific book, a theoretical book, or a practical book? It has to be noted that not all of the following rules apply to fiction, lyrical poetry, and plays, and there are different approaches to reading those kinds of books.

This does not mean that we cannot read these books analytically. And we will cover how to do that in another chapter. The following rules apply to expository books, being practical or theoretical books. Other books have slight differences, which we will identify along the way.

Rule 2 – Figure out what the book is about

This rule applies to all kinds of books. If it is a novel, you can clearly state the plot. If it is a theoretical book, you can summarize the theory it proposes. The main idea for this rule is to say what the whole book is about in one sentence, or at the most, one paragraph.

If you look at a research paper about any topic, you will come across an abstract at the beginning. You can see that the abstract clearly states what the research is about, how it is conducted, and what the results are. The second rule for figuring out the book's structure is similar.

Rule 3 – How the major parts of the book are organized

Now that you know what kind of book you have and what it is mainly about, you need to know how it is structured. And this is a very important aspect that tells you if the book is readable or unreadable because any good piece of writing should be unified, clear, and coherent.

Even if you can predict the plot of a novel, the main theory of a book, or what a practical book is trying to help you accomplish, the ideas within are complex and need to have a certain structure. Imagine that each argument the writer is putting forward is a house. A well-built city will have roads connecting those arguments, and everything needs to be clear to present an aerial view of the city. This is a well-written book. Now imagine a neglected neighborhood, where all of the houses are built randomly and nothing looks clear. This is the difference between a well-structured book and a poorly structured one.

Rule 4 – Getting to know the author's intentions

This is a critical step to knowing how the book is structured. If you already know the kind of book, what it is mainly about, and how it is divided, you might miss a big part of its structure if you aren't aware of why it is written in the first place. An analytical reader needs to know why this book has this structure, or else one would comprehend less its skeletal structure if they aren't aware of the end that the book serves.

However, it is also important not to fall into intentional fallacy, a term coined by William Wimsatt that argues that we should not evaluate a written work by making false assumptions about what the intention of the author was at the time of writing [14]. And honestly, we have no way of knowing so unless the author themself states it clearly somewhere.

The main idea of this rule is to figure out the problems laid out by the author, how they managed to present those problems and attempt to find a solution. Let us take this current book as an example. What was the intention of writing it? To lay down some ground rules that help readers become better readers. This does not assume that we know what the author had in mind while writing the book. We just need to understand their aim in writing the book.

Stage Two – The Book's Content

Every rule within this stage has two different steps. One concerns the language and grammar used, and the second concerns logic. And this is very crucial to understand when reading analytically because no language can be used without thought, and no thoughts can be communicated without using language.

Rule 5 - Find the important words, and come to terms with the author

Let us say you are trying to read a book by Sigmund Freud. You need to understand the important words used within his book and theories, which will allow you to come to terms with the author. This will help you to interpret the book's content.

You will find the words "id," "ego," and "superego" in Freud's book. An analytical reader needs to fully understand those words to be able to understand what Freud's psychoanalytical theory is about. So going to the trouble of finding the important words of a book will help you identify the meanings within and thus come to terms with what the author is saying.

The language part of this rule is to identify those words that are crucial to understanding the information and the logical thoughts laid out in the book.

Rule 6 – Find the most important sentences, and discover the propositions

We can already distinguish between a sentence and a proposition. But in this rule, the sentences are taken grammatically, while propositions are taken logically. We need to find out what the author is proposing in terms of ideas and arguments, and that can be found in the main grammatical sentences within the book.

Let us take as an example this sentence from Plato's *The Republic*, Book I, to fully understand the difference between a sentence and a proposition in the sense we are discussing:

There is nothing which for my part I like better, Cephalus, than conversing with aged men; for I regard them as travelers who have gone a journey which I too may have to go, and of whom I ought to enquire, whether the way is smooth and easy, or rugged and difficult [15].

Grammatically, this is a single sentence, but within this sentence, there are several propositions: (1) Socrates likes to converse with aged men; (2) he regards them as travelers who went through a long journey; (3) he thinks he might have to go through a similar journey; (4) he should enquire about this journey.

The key to understanding this sentence is to restate the propositions presented by the author in your own words. Once one is able to formulate a sentence to explain an idea, an argument, or a proposition laid out by someone else, then it can be safely assumed that they fully understand it.

Rule 7 – Construct the arguments and connect them to the sentences

The above sentence from Plato's book sets out a series of propositions. However, we still did not really get his main argument laid out in a series of sentences within his book. After finding the important sentences and extracting the main propositions, it is time to find the main arguments and locate the sentences where they are laid.

An argument can be proposed in a few sentences within a single paragraph, or it can run through several paragraphs. The analytical reader must understand those arguments and connect them to the sentences that explain them.

So the task of an analytical reader is to construct the arguments by finding the sentences and gathering them in a sequence that states the propositions composing that argument. And usually, authors make finding their main arguments relatively easy and put them together within a paragraph or two.

To sum up the first two stages of analytically reading a book: we can see that the reader goes from the book as a whole to the main arguments in stage one, then from the main words and sentences back up to those main arguments in stage two. Once these two processes are complete, a reader can then confidently say that they understand the contents of the book they are reading.

Rule 8 – Author's solutions

Now that a reader is fully aware of the book's contents and the end that the author is trying to achieve, the analytical reader can determine the solutions presented by the author. The German poet and critic Johann Wolfgang von Goethe outlined three questions for "constructive criticism" [16], and those are:

1. "What did the author set out to do?"
2. "Was his plan reasonable and sensible?"
3. "How far did he succeed in carrying it out?"

By answering those questions, the reader can determine the problems the author solved and those they didn't manage to solve. The analytical reader can also determine whether the author is aware that he didn't achieve all solutions.

This last rule of the second stage will open the door to the third and final stage of an analytical reading of a book. And that is the correct way to criticize it and give our opinions on what is written within. We can discuss those ideas, argue with the author, and in short, make a conversation with them.

Stage Three – Criticizing A Book

Now that the reader has analytically read the book, they have the right to have the last word. The author laid out everything they wanted to say within those pages, made their arguments, and clearly stated their points. The third stage is where the analytical reader converses with the book, thus indirectly with its author.

However, this conversation needs to be in order. The reader should be aware that there are rules to making that kind of conversation. After all, the authors of the book we read are not present to defend themselves. There are generally three maxims that need to be followed in order to converse properly with the author.

Rule 9 – Understand first, argue later

It is only fair to start the conversation with the author, that is to say, criticize the book, after fully understanding what they had to say. We cannot judge a book – agreeing or disagreeing with what it says – before comprehending what it says.

If a reader does not understand the book, the mere fact that they do not is criticism. If the reader believes it is the book's fault, this needs to be supported by arguments. Was it the structure of the book? Was it the way the author laid down the arguments? An analytical reader could pinpoint the cause of the incomprehension if he followed the rules mentioned.

But if the reader understands and agrees, then they have successfully read analytically, comprehended, and were further enlightened by what it said. When you understand and agree, your reading is completed. However, if you disagree, there are additional steps to consider before making a final judgment.

Rule 10 – Do not dispute or disagree contentiously

This goes without saying – be respectful, even if you disagree with what the author says. It brings nothing to you nor to the author to quarrel with the book in front of you. An analytical reader is sophisticated and intellectual. There are other ways to express your opinion and argue with the author than by being disputatious or contentious. This is the first principle of making an argument.

Let us take a book written by Frederic Nietzsche, you might disagree with some of the ideas he put forth because you hold a certain political position or a certain ideological stance, but that doesn't mean Nietzsche's book is useless to you. An analytical reader understands a book and pinpoints the common grounds, as well as the ideas on which they disagree with the author. Reading analytically and intelligently shouldn't lead to someone discarding a good book, regardless of whether the reader agrees or disagrees with every point made.

Rule 11 – Differ between your opinion and general knowledge

Of course, a reader can have an opinion about a topic. But if you want to argue, you need to make sure not to mix your own opinion or even the opinion of an author with general knowledge. Whatever claim is laid out, it needs to be backed by evidence or directly refuted. But an opinion about a matter can be argued, and a reader can either agree or disagree with what the author says.

The distinction between the two lies within the argument you are laying down. You need to present good reasons, backed by logic, for any position that you take.

The following rules are effective approaches in presenting such arguments.

Rule 12 – Pinpoint where the author is uninformed about what they are saying.

Rule 13 – Determine where the author is misinformed.

Rule 14 – Show where the author is illogical in what they are claiming.

Rule 15 – Identify if the author's analysis is incomplete.

Rules 12 to 15 are the concluding rules of analytical reading. They are the criteria that a reader needs to follow when making a critical judgment. When you disagree with an author, support your arguments with well-founded reasons. Did the author miss an important aspect regarding their discussion (uninformed)? Did they mention an incorrect fact (misinformed)? Were the author's arguments illogical? Was their analysis incomplete?

By following the three stages and the rules within each one, the analytical reader can answer fully and in detail the four main questions that would lead them to understand the book they are reading. And thus, a reader becomes a good reader, and can read a book in the best possible way to understand it.

Chart D Of The Levels Of Reading

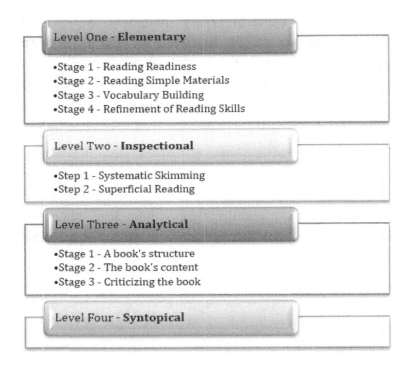

Level One - Elementary

- •Stage 1 - Reading Readiness
- •Stage 2 - Reading Simple Materials
- •Stage 3 - Vocabulary Building
- •Stage 4 - Refinement of Reading Skills

Level Two - Inspectional

- •Step 1 - Systematic Skimming
- •Step 2 - Superficial Reading

Level Three - Analytical

- •Stage 1 - A book's structure
- •Stage 2 - The book's content
- •Stage 3 - Criticizing the book

Level Four - Syntopical

Level Four – Syntopical Reading

As mentioned earlier, the fourth level of reading is practically reading several books analytically. The whole goal of syntopical reading is to have a certain subject in mind and group all those books related to the subject they are trying to solve. A syntopical reader can come up with an analysis of a certain subject that may not be found in any of the books that they are reading.

And this is why a student writing a dissertation needs to read syntopically. Regardless of their topic or even their major of study, a Ph.D. student needs to add an idea, notion, theory, or new argument to the existing literature on the topic in mind. What they first need to do, is to find all of the books that already discussed their topic, read them analytically, and come up with their point of view on that topic. They might agree with a few points found in those books, and disagree with others.

Whether writing a dissertation or not, reading at a syntopical level is the most rewarding activity for a reader can do. The many benefits that the intellectual mind can derive make it worth learning how to achieve this level of reading.

The first thing one needs to do is to locate several books on the subject in mind. And to effectively do so, the reader needs to read several books on an inspectional level to make that decision. Once you have a number of books in front of you and you are certain that they discuss the subject that you need, there are five steps you need to follow to read syntopically [17].

Step 1 – Find The Relevant Passages

In contrast to analytical reading, reading at this level will put your concerns, intentions, and goals before the authors'. You can, of course, go through each book individually and read each one on the third level of reading. However, in this case, you will be placing the book and its author first, and the problem you're researching second.

The subject and the problem that you are posing is the main goal of this level of reading. You will need to inspect all the books in front of you to identify the passages relevant to your queries and your concerns. You should not confuse this type of inspection with the first inspection mentioned earlier. The first type is aimed at finding out if the book is relevant to your subject matter in the first place. Once you have the books you know are relevant in front of you, you need to inspect them again in terms of what you need to solve your problem.

Of course, an experienced reader can do both simultaneously. So while I am inspecting a book to see if it fits my subject, and I find that it does, I can automatically start finding the relevant passages that discuss the subject I have in mind.

Step 2 – Bring The Authors To Terms

In the second stage of analytical reading and most particularly in rule 5, we needed to come to terms with the author after locating the important words they used in their book. However, when faced with several authors, they might not have used the same words or even the same terms. In this case, it is your job to establish those terms and bring the authors to them.

In this step, you force the authors to use your language, and you do not have to necessarily use theirs. If you do accept the terminology of one author, you will very likely be lost and your own questions will get confused with what a particular author is trying to solve. So you must, to some extent, think of syntopical reading as a sort of translation exercise. It is your terms, your questions, and your solutions that you aim at, and not any of the other authors.

<u>Step 3 – Get The Questions Clear</u>

Just like we have to locate the propositions laid out by an author when we are analytically reading a book, in syntopical reading, we need to lay out our own propositions. We need to set out questions and put them in an order that helps the reader figure out a solution for the problem they outlined. We also need to formulate those questions so that the authors of our chosen books have the answers somewhere. The main difficulty of this step is that those are your questions about the subject you are tackling and the authors may not have asked them.

Let us take as an example Michel Foucault's *Madness and Civilization: A History of Insanity in the Age of Reason*. This book was actually Foucault's own doctoral thesis. His main questions revolved around madness and its role in Western society [18]. If you get the chance to read the book, you will see that Foucault traced the concept of madness – which was his main subject – across several cultures in Western society.

He read many history books, novels, and biographies of authors and famous people deemed insane at a certain time. Not all of the books he read to compile an answer for how the concept of madness has evolved might even touch upon his subject matter. The author of a history book might not have that subject in mind when detailing a certain period. But Foucault came out with his own concepts, terms, and theory on the subject by posing the right questions, and finding the answers in all the literature he read.

So what kind of questions can we ask? And in what order? Of course, this all goes to the subject you choose, but there are a few general guidelines for the order of the questions [19]:

1. The first questions concern the phenomenon or the main idea that the reader is investigating.
2. If an author mentions the idea, we can further ask how this idea manifests itself.
3. Finally, we can ask about the consequences of the answers we have found so far.

It must be noted that not all authors will answer all of the questions, or even if they do, they might not answer them in the same way. Since each author gave their own opinion and own answers, it is the reader's task to come to a consensus.

Step 4 – Define The Issues

If you pose the right questions, and several authors answer the questions in a different way, then an issue arises about the subject.It is the syntopical reader's job to define that issue. Those authors didn't converse with each other. You are bringing them together and making them "discuss" the problem that you have posed.

It is very rare to find simply two opposing fronts about a subject. You will, in fact, find several different answers and viewpoints regarding the subject of your choice. This is because the question asked in the first place has different conceptions from each of the authors. You have to keep in mind that, while writing their book, the authors did not ask the questions you are asking. So a syntopical reader needs to define the issues, and one might find many controversial aspects of the subject.

You might find that no author has already located such controversies or posed the questions you're asking. So it is the reader's job to sort out and arrange those controversies and the issues to come up with a discussion.

Step 5 – Analyze The Discussion

In the first four steps of a syntopical reading, we have so far done the following:

1. Located the relevant passages
2. Created our own terminology and applied it to all of the authors
3. Posed some questions in a certain order
4. Defined the issues produced by the authors' answers to those questions.

The only thing left to do is to ask two additional questions: "Is this true?" and "what of it?" [20], just like we ask in an analytical reading after understanding the book. The only difference, in this case, is to ask and answer the questions in a specific order and defend that particular order. We should show the different answers to the questions and be able to say why it is so. We must also be able to locate the specific passages in the books in support of that order. Only then, will we be able to say that we have properly analyzed the discussion regarding the problem.

A correct and thorough analysis might produce more benefits than simply coming up with a conclusion. We could end up creating the groundwork for a new work that discusses that specific problem. In fact, if you think about it, without syntopical reading, we wouldn't have had so many books in the first place, filled with so many ideas that seem to build on each other continuously.

Chart E Of The Levels Of Reading

Level One - Elementary

- Stage 1 - Reading Readiness
- Stage 2 - Reading Simple Materials
- Stage 3 - Vocabulary Building
- Stage 4 - Refinement of Reading Skills

Level Two - Inspectional

- Step 1 - Systematic Skimming
- Step 2 - Superficial Reading

Level Three - Analytical

- Stage 1 - A book's structure
- Stage 2 - The book's content
- Stage 3 - Criticizing the book

Level Four - Syntopical

- Step 1 - Find the relevant passages
- Step 2 - Bring the authors to terms
- Step 3 - Get the questions clear
- Step 4 - Define the issues
- Step 5 - Analyze the discussion

Action Steps

The following exercises revolve around the second and third levels of reading. You are, of course, free to choose whatever book that interests you to practice reading at either an inspectional or analytical level. The exercises below are mere suggestions. But it is advised that you practice the second level prior to the third one.

If you prefer to choose your own books to read on both of those levels, think of a topic, head to the local library, and try to find a couple of books about that topic that interests you. First, read them at the second level, that is to say, skim through them, read a few parts, and decide which book you would like to take home. Once you decide on a book, try to follow the three stages and the rules to read the book of your choice analytically.

<u>Exercises</u>

I – Check out the contents page and preface of the book *Critical Thinking: The Art of Argument* written by George W. Rainbolt and Sandra L. Dwyer.

1. Determine the type of book. Is it practical or theoretical?
2. How are the book's contents organized?
3. What were the authors' intentions in writing this book?

This exercise refers to the first step of inspectional reading as well as part of the first stage of analytical reading.

II – Grab the last novel you have read. Inspect it again – skim through it as in the second level of reading. Try to see how its contents are divided, and try to state the plot of the novel in a sentence or, at most, a paragraph. Determine the major parts of that plot as you go over the book quickly and see how they are organized.

This exercise will also help in practicing inspectional reading as well as applying the second and third rules of analytical reading.

III – Take the time to pick up a book to read it analytically. Make sure it is an expository book and not fictional, to apply all of the rules. Choose a book that you have already read to practice applying the rules. As you get more comfortable with applying the steps and rules, try to read a new book analytically.

Note down your analysis of the book after you fully understand it:

1. What are the author's problems and solutions?
2. Do you agree or disagree with the author?
3. On which points do you disagree with the author?
4. Why do you disagree with the author?

Remember always to provide evidence that supports your opinion.

Summary

All four siblings, the teacher, the med student, the psychologist, and the Ph.D. student, read or deal with reading, but each one reads on a different level. And if you think about it, every level requires knowing and excelling at the skills needed to read at a previous level. Everyone knows how to read at an elementary level, of course. Jane, the psychologist, already knows how to read at the inspectional level, which allows her to choose the particular book she needs to read analytically. And Jack definitely knows how to read analytically to read syntopically. All the levels of reading are cumulative, and one cannot move from one level to the next without becoming an expert at their current level. Once you can practice reading at higher levels, one question remains. How can a good reader keep the information and retain it properly?

Key Takeaways

There are four different levels of reading.

Level one – Elementary reading:

- Stage 1 - Reading readiness
- Stage 2 - Reading simple material
- Stage 3 - Vocabulary building
- Stage 4 - Refinement of reading skills

Level two – Inspectional reading

- Step 1 – skimming or pre-reading – this is where a reader takes a quick look at a book and is able to understand the kind of book it is, its topic, and its main structure.
- Step 2 – Superficial reading – reading a book from start to finish without stopping to ponder or think about the details.

Level three – Analytical reading

- Stage 1 – The structure of the book – find the kind of book you're reading, its major parts and its organization – and determine the questions that the author poses.

- Stage 2 – The contents of the book – start with finding the words and sentences to come to terms with the author and figure out the propositions made. You can then construct the author's arguments and determine if they were successful in solving their problem.
- Stage 3 – Criticizing the book – make sure you understand the book before judging, do not be contentious, and differentiate between knowledge and your personal opinion. Show in your criticism if an author is uninformed, misinformed, illogical, or if their analysis is incomplete.

Level four – Syntopical reading

Determine a topic and inspect several books to pick the relevant ones

- Step 1 – Find the relevant passages in terms of your own concerns and not the authors'.
- Step 2 – Create neutral terminology and bring the author to your terms.
- Step 3 – Create the questions and put them in the correct order.
- Step 4 – Define the issues that arise from the authors answering your questions.
- Step 5 – Start a conversation and analyze the discussion created from your questions.

6

THE ART OF LITERARY INTERPRETATIONS

HOW TO APPLY YOUR EXPERIENCES AND KNOWLEDGE TO GAIN MORE INSIGHTS

During literature test...

Derp reads the following question:

What did the writer mean when he wrote "the sky was blue":
a) Sadness
b) Hope
c) Infinite happiness
d) Carpe Diem

HE MEANT THAT THE SKY IS FREAKING BLUE!!!!

The Sky Is Blue

This meme depicts a common joke that many of us might have used in English classes in high school. When the teacher asked us to interpret a poem, novel, or any literary text, many of us found it funny that they were overinterpreting the author's words. Meanwhile, the author might not have even thought about any of that. And we can imagine them sitting and reading an analysis of their texts saying, "So that's what I meant!! Interesting!"

Before going into how to retain information within the text, there is an essential aspect of reading to discuss. And that is literary interpretation. Although we all did try to interpret texts back in high school, most of us came out of it by making memes like the above. This is because many fall into the trap of trying to find meaning in a text by explaining the intentions of the author in such a way that it leads to an excavation of the work going way deeper than necessary [1].

However, literary interpretation is a very important aspect, when done correctly. And a good reader needs to be aware of what literary interpretation is, why it is useful when reading a book, and how to interpret a text to read it better.

A Tale As Old As Time

The Greek philosopher Aristotle lived almost three hundred years before Christ. He attempted in his work *Poetics* to understand how drama worked and its effects on the audience. Many studies after Aristotle focused on the relationship between life and literature. Now there is an abundance of schools of criticism and literary theories specifically dedicated to criticizing and interpreting a text. In science, having a new theory usually displaces its precedent, but this rarely happens in literary theories [2].

The notion of literary theory started with theories about the structure and form of a text in the twenties and thirties [3]. However, we now have theories that encompass as many fields as one can think of: from political theories like the Marxist theory to psychological theories. There are theories about gender studies, ethnic and indigenous studies, postcolonial theories, evolutionary literary theory, and there is even recent talk about "the death of theory," which might just end up being another theory in itself.

If we want to consider the nature of theory, well, it is technically "a way of thinking." Theoretical thinking is actually itself a paradigm of thought. It is used to understand ideas and concepts and combine them meaningfully [4].

Discussing literary theories will require room to fill another book; however, it remains to ask what is the point of literary theories and literary interpretation, and how might they help us read better?

What Is Literary Interpretation?

If you've read so far, you know that reading better and understanding more of a book requires that the good reader asks questions. And when discussing literary interpretation, there are questions that also need to be asked. The critical mind of a reader should attempt to examine the following very broad questions in literary interpretation [5]:

- How does this book make sense?
- What kind of sense does it make?
- Why does it make sense in a particular way rather than the other?

Those questions are slightly different from those we ask when reading critically, analytically, or syntopically. However, asking the right questions for literary interpretation is as important to reading better. And the main aim of literary interpretation is to find meaning in the book. However, when you read and interpret, the task is not about finding the right meaning within a text, but it is the "process of creating meaning" [6].

You might be wondering how a reader can create meaning for an existing text which supposedly has a meaning. Well, this is where the importance of literary interpretation lies.

Importance Of Literary Interpretation

Back in 1912, William Shakespeare's play *The Tragedy of Hamlet, Prince of Denmark* was interpreted according to the Oedipus tragedy of Sophocles. In his article entitled *Current Literature of Psychoanalysis*, Dr. J.S. Van Teslar argues that Hamlet rests on a fantasy of incest. He relates the rivalry between Hamlet and his father to the state of the family at the time. He argues that this goes back to the matriarchal form of family organization and clan marriage. And he adds that this is why incest fantasies are found in mythologies [7].

Some sixty years later, in 1975, Theodore Lidz, a professor of psychiatry at Yale University, argues in his book that Hamlet is clinically termed as mad. This is because of mood swings that lead him to depression, judgment impairment, and disillusions[8].

Fast forward another forty and some years, in 2020, Rhodri Lewis argues that Hamlet has a philosophical depth and that he "sees through the manifest corruption of personal and political life." He adds that Shakespeare's tragic hero has a penetrating vision that joins an optimism about the human condition with an "existential nausea" [9].

Of course, there are many more interpretations of Shakespeare's Hamlet going back to the 17th century. Those different interpretations come from various historical periods and readers from distinct social groups. And this is precisely why no singular objective meaning can be determined solely by the text. This variation in interpretation means that a text's meaning depends on the social circumstances of when the text is created and interpreted, as well as what readers add to it.

The importance of literary interpretation goes even further. It does not only affect the way readers or critics view the rhetoric of a given text. In fact, such rhetoric also contributes to creating meanings in society and helps in its circulation within that society. We actually understand the world along with our place within the world through those texts that we create and then interpret [10].

The Book Is Now Yours

Interpreting a book or any text is making it your own. You add your own views to the written text and argue in defense of your interpretation. That book you read and interpret becomes part of the society you live in, as it becomes part of your world. So how can someone make a literary interpretation without trying to figure out why is the sky blue?

Such a question goes back to the already-mentioned notion of "intentional fallacy." English teachers asked us in high school, "What do you think the author means?" The issue here lies with the fact that authors can never completely free their own texts from ambiguity. In fact, literary interpretation goes much further than what the author means. We have freedom in our interpretations as long as we are able to support our views [11].

Noticeably, none of the above-mentioned interpretations of Hamlet were concerned with what Shakespeare meant. A character in a novel, a play, a poem, or any literary text is separated from the text's narrator and the author's feelings.

The characters are the creations of the authors but do not necessarily reflect their views. Otherwise, Thomas Hardy's *Tess of the D'Urberville*, for instance, couldn't exist, since the author is a male and the heroine is a female. Even if the text uses the first person, the speaker should be regarded as a separate entity from the author [12].

Literary Interpretation

As mentioned earlier, the reader needs to ask a set of questions to interpret a text properly. Usually, most such questions should come by naturally while you are reading. Good readers will question while reading, answers will begin to form, and then they will start making connections with other texts as well as with their own personal views.

The questions below are a few of the many that could lead the reader into a line of inquiry to follow about a particular text [13]:

About the text

1. Is this text a part of a larger text, or is it complete?
2. Are there more versions of the text? How are they different?
3. Was the text edited? Is it translated?

About the context

1. When and where was the text produced, and under what circumstances?
2. Who was the intended audience of the text?

3. Is the author a male or a female? And how old were they when they wrote the text?

About the speakers

1. Who is speaking in the text?
2. Whose point of view is reflected?
3. Who is the addressee of that text?

About the language

1. Do all the words used in the text still have the same meanings as they did when the text was written?
2. Are the sentences within the text uniform in length and complexity? If not, is there a specific reason for that?
3. Do different speakers use different dialects or ways of expression within the text?

About the symbols

1. Are the names used in the text refer to certain types of characters?
2. Do locations and setting within the text symbolize something?
3. Does the text's title convey a key meaning?

About the representation

1. Does the text represent the time and place of its publication, or is it untypical in terms of its themes?
2. Does the text represent any socially core themes (racism, women's issues, success, fulfillment, etc.)? If it does, do you see them as unjust or biased?
3. Are the topics discussed new to you?

About your experience

1. Do you find any aspects of yourself within the characters or events?
2. Does anything that happens in the text resonate with your own experience?
3. Are there any parts within the text that offend, repel, or embarrass you?

To Read Better

The questions above are suggestions and starting points for what you might find and question about a book while reading. The most practical way to use this set of questions is to first read the text and then take a look at the questions to see if there are any questions you might answer. In many instances, you would not use or need all of those questions. It all depends on the text that you are reading.

After going over the questions, one of them might lead you to take notice of a detail that you've missed within the text. You will then need to go back and read the text again to start answering the questions. All of your answers will have a sort of reasoning that you start to think about consciously [14]. Once you go over all of the questions, review those that engaged you most, leading you to the literary interpretation of the text.

Action Steps

I – Read the following poem:

"The White Man's Burden"

Take up the White Man's burden—

Send forth the best ye breed—

Go send your sons to exile

To serve your captives' need

To wait in heavy harness

On fluttered folk and wild—

Your new-caught, sullen peoples,

Half devil and half child.

Take up the White Man's burden

In patience to abide

To veil the threat of terror

And check the show of pride;

By open speech and simple

An hundred times made plain

To seek another's profit

And work another's gain.

Take up the White Man's burden—

And reap his old reward:

The blame of those ye better

The hate of those ye guard—

The cry of hosts ye humour

(Ah slowly) to the light:

"Why brought ye us from bondage,

"Our loved Egyptian night?"

Take up the White Man's burden-

Have done with childish days-

The lightly proffered laurel,

The easy, ungrudged praise.

Comes now, to search your manhood

Through all the thankless years,

Cold-edged with dear-bought wisdom,

The judgment of your peers!

II – Skim the questions above, and determine which ones you find are relevant to the text. Note down the most important questions that go into your mind and try to answer them without having any context about the poem.

III – The author of this poem is Rudyard Kipling. Read the circumstances of writing that poem below.

"In November 1898, Rudyard Kipling sent his poem "The White Man's Burden" to his friend Theodore Roosevelt, who had just been elected Governor of New York .Kipling's aim was to encourage the American government to take over the Philippines, one of the territorial prizes of the Spanish-American War, and rule it with the same energy, honor, and beneficence that, he believed, characterized British rule over the nonwhite populations of India and Africa. In September he had written to Roosevelt: "Now go in and put all the weight of your influence into hanging on permanently to the whole Philippines. America has gone and stuck a pickaxe into the foundations of a rotten house and she is morally bound to build the house over again from the foundations or have it fall about her ears" [15].

Does your interpretation change regarding some of the questions?

IV- Read more about the poem's setting and the criticism that came afterward in this short article, "'The White Man's Burden' and Its Critics" by Jim Zwick.[16] What do you think of Mark Twain's statement two years later when he said, "The White Man's Burden has been sung. Who will sing the Brown Man's?"

Summary

Literary interpretation helps readers read better. Back in high school, we all read texts closely, and we can still use a good interpretation while reading outside of the classroom. A good reader should always ask the important questions when facing a written book, and literary interpretation is no different. With the right questions in mind, and with answers that you can logically defend, you might figure out a meaning out of the text that even the author hasn't thought about while writing. Literary interpretation is what makes a book timeless. Regardless of how many centuries ago a book was written, good readers can relate it to their time and circumstances by creating new meaning.

<u>Key Takeaways</u>

- Literary interpretation is about figuring out the answers to the below questions:

1. How does this book make sense?
2. What kind of sense does it make?
3. Why does it make sense in a particular way rather than the other?

- Reading is not the task of finding the right meaning within a text, but it is the process of creating meaning.
- A text's meaning depends on the social

circumstances of when the text is created and interpreted, as well as what readers add to it.

- The questions you ask when you read a text will revolve around the text itself, its context, the speakers, the language used within the text, the symbols, how it is represented, and how it relates to you.
- Not all of the questions apply to all texts. Literary interpretation is about answering questions related to the text and finding meaning in it that relates to you.

7

AFTER READING COMES REMEMBERING

DISCOVER THE TECHNIQUES THAT CAN HELP YOU RETAIN KNOWLEDGE AND INSIGHTS FROM READING

"I Can't Quite Recall What It Said"

"It's been a while since we haven't had the chance to catch up!" says Tony while sipping his cup of coffee and looking at his childhood friend Ian who is busy adding the third spoon of sugar to his own cup.

"You mean face-to-face! Oh man, that pandemic took a toll on us!" replies Ian as he is mixing his coffee and taking a sip to see if it is sweet enough.

"I can't believe you still add that much sugar. It's bad for you. Plus, you never know with the current situation, things might get so much worse that we won't be able to find any," says Toni somberly.

"Hey! Cheer up, buddy. I know there are loads of issues going on, you know the Russian-Ukrainian war, the aftermath of the pandemic, the political turmoil we're living in, the current price surge... But that still doesn't mean we're doomed to lose our sugar!" Ian laughs while trying in vain to find a positive aspect of the past couple of years they've lived through.

"Yeah, well, who would have thought we'd be fighting over toilet paper a couple of years back? By the way, did you hear any news from Jeremy? I heard he was diagnosed with chronic depression."

"Yeah! This is getting serious. Honestly, we all are in a slump—believe it or not—just by trying to keep up. At least we still have our jobs! The whole world is in depression!" Ian raises his hands in despair.

"You know, I just remembered I read a book about that during the lockdown. It was, in fact, entitled *The World in Depression*, mainly discussing the reasons for the lost decade that started in the 1930s," says Toni while taking another sip.

"That's interesting! Well, what were the reasons? Maybe we'd learn from history for once," inquires Ian while leaning forward in interest.

"There were many theories about it. Some say it started in Europe; some declare it is the inflation in the US. There was actually a very interesting egg and chicken question about what came first.... I really can't recall what it said really, but it was something about the financial state at the time. I remember it sounded really similar to what we're going through," says Toni hesitantly.

Ian leans back in comfort in his chair again and sarcastically answers, "Yeah, it sounds really interesting. It would have been enlightening indeed... Maybe I should read the book."

"You should. It is really interesting!"

"If you'd remembered though, that conversation would have gone somewhere!" teases Ian and they laugh together and take another sip.

How Our Brains Function

How many times have we faced similar issues? We have read something of interest and we'd love to share it with others, yet we cannot seem to recall all of the details! The purpose of this book is to read better. To read better, we need to understand better what we read. But what is the point of understanding if we cannot recall the information?

Scientists categorize memories according to how long they last within our minds: immediate memories last for milliseconds, working memories last for around a minute, and long-term memories last from an hour to several years. Since our aim is to retain the information we read, we need to put the information in our long-term memory. After all, this is how we are able to recall the information.

Consolidation is the term used for the process of converting working memories to long-term memories. In practice, we can achieve this best if we learn the information in a context that we comprehend or if it is emotionally significant for us [1]. Accordingly, how would Toni have remembered this part from the book he read?

"... Like the First World War, the Napoleonic Wars were followed by a short, sharp deflation in 1816, comparable to that of 1920-21, and a period of monetary adjustment culminating in the restoration of the pound to par in 1819 and 1821. Then came a spurt of foreign lending from 1821 to 1825, followed by a stock market crash in 1826 and a depression. If one subtracts 100 plus three to five years from the major economic events of the 1920s and 1930s, interesting parallels emerge. The 1826 depression was not perhaps as deep or as widespread as that of 1929 or as those of 1837 and 1848 that followed it. But the timing is disconcertingly similar" [2].

Toni would have easily remembered all of the details in this passage if he truly understood the context or if it was emotionally significant to him. So, he would be able to recall the information if he knew a lot about economics or if his grandfather, let's say, lost all of his fortunes during the depression. But what if Toni isn't an Economics expert, nor is he emotionally connected to what he reads?

We first need to be aware of how our memories function to find the correct ways to give them the boost they need to achieve memory consolidation. We also need to take into account the limitations our memories have. The human brain has the capacity to remember a lot of information in exquisite detail, yet it is not good, for instance, at recalling lengthy lists of unrelated numbers and many meaningless words.

How can we achieve memory consolidation when reading new information? We need to focus our learning strategies on the strengths of our memory systems within our brains [3]. So, we can create emotional arousal for what we read (e.g., the book's topic might be something we really care about), or we can put it in a context that we truly understand.

Your Way To Absorb Information

Learning is an individual process, and many variables affect the way we each learn, from our experiences to our personality traits. Before delving into the techniques that we can use to strengthen our memory's function and learn retention techniques, we first need to know the different cognitive learning styles and identify which one works best for each of us. Those cognitive learning styles refer to how people prefer to receive new information that they process, absorb, and recall successfully [4]. Once one identifies and starts using their own preferred cognitive learning style, they put the ideas in a context that they understand.

<u>Identify Your Personal Technique</u>

There are three kinds of learners: visual, auditory, and kinesthetic [5]. When you use your personal learning technique to process new information, you will be able to learn more efficiently and recall information much more smoothly. Although learning styles are not definitive and are sometimes subjective to certain conditions, it is worth trying to identify the one you feel helps you remember better.

Visual Learners - As a child, a visual learner would usually be fascinated with colors, shapes, picture books, and animations. All visual learners remember best when they see or visualize information. They mostly have a keen awareness of the beauty of the world and of aesthetics. Visual learners are able to easily understand and recall information shown in pictures, diagrams, and charts, or they usually create a mental image of the information.

Auditory Learners - Since childhood, an auditory learner would be seen as someone who talks nonstop, constantly sings nursery rhymes, and loves to ask questions. They usually have a good ear for music, strong linguistic skills, and great oral communication skills. They learn by listening to others explain something, and they most often get involved in discussions because they can remember the information by explaining it in their own words.

Kinesthetic Learners - A young kinesthetic learner would have been always full of energy; they'd constantly be running, jumping, taking things apart, and trying to build new things. They can rarely sit still, work well with their hands, and usually have a good sense of body movements and timing. Kinesthetic learners learn by pacing around when reading or listening to new information, using hand gestures, or by working standing up on a chalkboard or other large surfaces.

Techniques To Retain Information

Many of the strategies below involve using more than one learning style. But benefiting from more sensory channels to process the information would create a stronger impression of the information in your memory, and you'll thus be able to recall that information more quickly [6]. However, once you identify your cognitive learning technique, you'd be able to focus on the sensory channel that suits you best.

Before going over each technique, we need to be fully aware of the information that we need to retain. Of course, as a reader, you are not aiming at remembering every detail within a book. Usually, a detail or an example given within the book sticks in our memories, because we can relate to it and it has aroused our emotions. But there are facts that are important to recall even if we do not get emotionally attached to them.

We have already covered the levels of reading, and noted that the best reading one can achieve is analytical reading. In this level of reading, the reader mainly attempts to answer questions that revolve around the book's theme and how the author organizes the main ideas, arguments, and conclusions. And the answers to those questions will mostly contain the information that is worthy of being in our long-term memory.

Taking Notes

When you are reading a book, and want to retain the information within, a good way to do so is by taking notes. While reading on the analytical level, the second stage involves finding the important words to interpret the content, constructing the author's arguments, and connecting them to the most important sentences. This stage is a good place to start taking notes, which will help you retain as well as complete the third stage successfully (criticizing the book).

Taking notes is a good way to remember because whenever you write something down, it ends up being sealed in your memory. Generally, the notes should be the answers to the main questions that the reader is asking while reading the book. Your notes should generally be about [7]:

- Identifying and explaining the key terms.
- Listing down the main ideas.
- Listing down all major supporting arguments but not the minor ones.

An example of note-taking is the "Key Takeaways" section of every chapter within this book. While you are reading, you should aim at taking notes of the main ideas in a similar way.

However, sometimes a book offers many ideas that a mere list might be an understatement of what the book is discussing. In this case, making an outline will be more helpful. Outlines have more structure than notes do, and they will help the reader remember the ideas and the relationship between them. An outline should mostly look something like this [8]:

I. Topic or Subject

A. Main idea

1. Major supporting argument

a. Minor supporting argument

b.

c.

2. Another major supporting argument

a. Minor supporting argument

b.

c.

And so on. Sometimes a book might tackle more than one topic or subject under the umbrella of a larger theme. Writing down an outline in this way will help in organizing all the ideas and connecting them.

Note-taking can be a good tool for all three types of learners. A visual learner will imprint the image of the outline or notes in their memory for retention. An auditory learner can read them aloud while or after writing them down. A kinesthetic learner can write them on a board, or write each one on a piece of paper. They can then move around the papers on a desk to connect them. The trick is to use exaggerated hand gestures to help in retention.

Reiteration

If Toni had called Ian right after he read the book, or even right after the passage he found interesting and told him about it in his own words, he would be able to remember those details two years later. Sharing the information you find with someone else is a great way to keep it in your long-term memory and is another technique for retention.

This method helps in memory consolidation because it is all about repeating the information again and again, which solidifies it in your long-term memory. To successfully work on this technique, the reader will need to reiterate the information as many times as possible. But there are mainly three general stages that the reader needs to go through [9]:

1. After reading, the first reiteration is about repeating the ideas in your own words. When you know that you might want to share the ideas with someone, you'll start practicing the way you will need to communicate the ideas. You might need to go back to the book at this stage and double-check that you fully understand it. If you do not, you will not be able to formulate it in your own words clearly.

2. This stage of reiteration can be repeated as many times as needed. Once you successfully repeat the ideas on your

own with the book in hand, you will need to practice repeating them again and again afterward without the book. This will help you keep the information in mind and ensure that you know exactly what you would say when you eventually meet someone with whom you want to share the ideas.

3. The next stage is to actually share the information with someone. Once you do, that person might ask you some questions. This interaction is a great way to help you think deeper into what you've read and helps you to understand it thoroughly.

Sharing the information is a magnificent way to understand as well as retain what you have read. And the fact that you want to share something with someone and discuss it will be an added motive for your retention.

You can repeat each one of those reiteration stages as many times as needed, including sharing the information with many people at different intervals. This will also be a chance to discuss the ideas with different people, adding new perspectives to your reading. Someone might ask a question that hasn't occurred to you, which will add to the joy of reading and gaining knowledge.

How can different learners reiterate? Obviously, the auditory learner can summarize the ideas and say them aloud. A visual learner can draw charts and diagrams while practicing reiteration, and the information will be mirrored by a mental image in their brains. A kinesthetic learner can say them aloud while pacing back and forth, while driving, or by writing them down.

Creating Mind Maps

Tony Buzan introduced the idea of mind maps in the 1960s [10]. It helps readers to extract successfully the main ideas from a book, connect them in a way that the reader understands, and ultimately helps in memory consolidation.

A mind map is a diagram that contains words, ideas, and items that are arranged and linked to a central keyword or idea [11]. Buzan defines mind maps as follows:

"A mind map harnesses the full range of cortical skills — word, image, number, logic, rhythm, color, and spatial awareness — in a single, uniquely powerful technique. In doing so, it gives you the freedom to roam the infinite expanse of your brain." [12]

The following figure is an example of a mind map [13].

As you can see, it is about time management, and if you do not fully understand it, it is because each mind map is personal, and only the creator fully understands it — unless they explain it to you. If this is the first time you are introduced to a mind map, you might be wondering: what use would it help a reader to take the time to draw such a map since there are other techniques? Well, this technique encompasses both of the previous ones. You will not be able to create it if you haven't taken a few notes to rely on, and you can practice reiteration by reviewing the mind map.

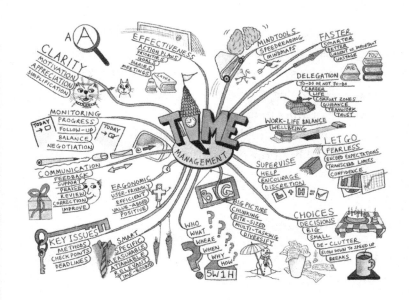

Advantages of creating a mind map

Below are a few advantages to using a mind map [14]:

- The process of creating it is much more interesting and more fun than simply writing down the ideas, creating tables, or making standard charts.
- The mind map's visual quality assists the creator in identifying, clarifying, classifying, summarizing, consolidating, highlighting, and presenting the structural ideas of a subject in a much simpler way than standard notes.
- Most importantly, a mind map facilitates recalling the information because the associations created mirror the way our brain

functions. It is actually much easier to remember images and keywords than lengthy notes.

- Mind maps are concise, include no unnecessary words, are very flexible, and can include several pages of information.
- A mind map can identify gaps in information and shed light on crucial issues.

How to create a mind map

There are three main steps to creating a mind map [15]:

1. Identify the keywords – which we already do in a good reading.

2. Create main branches from those keywords – where you would put in more words that lead you to remember the ideas around the keywords.

3. Draw simple icons for each word and use colors. (optional)

This chapter's key takeaways are listed down as a mind map for your reference in creating one. All learners will generally enjoy creating a mind map. A visual learner will recall how it looks, an auditory learner will remember better by saying the keywords and creating sentences to explain the connections, while a kinesthetic learner can follow the branches with his hands while going over the map.

Action Plan

If you have recently read anything that interests you, whether a book or an article, you can try out all three techniques to practice information retention.

As a suggestion, you can check out the book Toni has read, *The World in Depression, 1929-1939*,[16] and read the introduction.

- Make use of note-taking, outlining, reiteration, and drawing a mind map while reading. You do not have to put all the information found in the introduction in your notes or mind map.
- Practice the techniques to see if you could get the conversation between Toni and Ian to go further.
- Once you are done, try talking about it with someone and telling them what you have read without referring to your notes.

Some questions to consider regarding what to aim at for retention:

- What are the general reasons that economists believe are the causes of the world depression of 1930?
- What are the two main theories in the debate?
- Can you explain the egg and chicken question that Toni tried to explain?

Summary

Although Toni was excited to share the information he read in the book, he was not able to do so. This is because he couldn't promptly recall the important information he had read. Being able to remember is an essential part of reading a book better. What use was it for Toni to read and understand the book if later on, he was unable to make use of and share the knowledge he learned?

It is important that each reader understands how their brain functions and how to give their memories the boost it needs to make better use of the retention techniques. Another important aspect of reading well is building reading vocabulary. A book about reading cannot end without touching on this important issue, which will be the following chapter's focus.

<u>Key Takeaways</u>

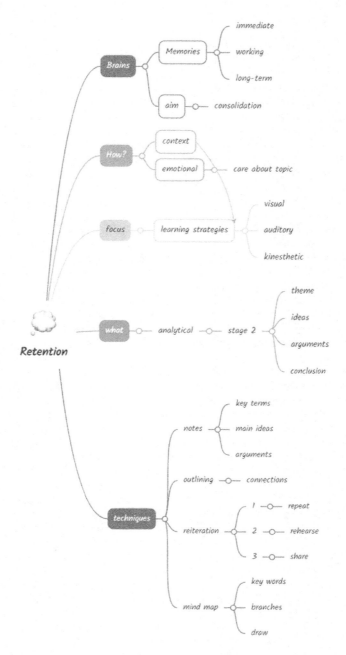

Retention

Brains
- Memories
  - immediate
  - working
  - long-term
- aim
  - consolidation

How?
- context
- emotional
  - care about topic

focus
- learning strategies
  - visual
  - auditory
  - kinesthetic

what
- analytical
  - stage 2
    - theme
    - ideas
    - arguments
    - conclusion

techniques
- notes
  - key terms
  - main ideas
  - arguments
- outlining
  - connections
- reiteration
  - 1 — repeat
  - 2 — rehearse
  - 3 — share
- mind map
  - key words
  - branches
  - draw

8

MASTERING VOCABULARY

LEARN THE APPROACHES TO TURN JARGONS TO COMMON WORDS

A Small Drop Of Ink

> *But words are things, and a small drop of ink,*
>
> *Falling like dew, upon a thought, produces*
>
> *That which makes thousands, perhaps millions, think;*
>
> *'T is strange, the shortest letter which man uses*
>
> *Instead of speech, may form a lasting link*
>
> *Of ages; to what straits old Time reduces*
>
> *Frail man, when paper--even a rag like this,*
>
> *Survives himself, his tomb, and all that's his."*
>
> —Lord Byron, Don Juan, Canto III

Elizabeth closes the book and ponders about what she read. She has always loved reading and this part has left her wondering about the activity's essence, "such a small drop of ink makes thousands, perhaps millions think." It is true. Words are magic, she thought, everlasting. They are what make books timeless. It is all about the words. She smiles as she feels herself thinking by using words! What would we be without words? How do animals communicate without words? It is what sets us apart, what makes us rule the earth!

How many words are there? How many word combinations can we make? This simple idea fascinated her! How many more words are there that I do not know about? She frowns. How would I know if there is a word I do not know? She stands up and walks toward her bookshelf. She picks up the dictionary. While holding it, she looks at it in bewilderment. It is huge! She puts it aside, takes out her phone, and googles, "How big is the Oxford dictionary?" Twenty-two thousand pages. Six hundred thousand words. She was mesmerized. I do not think anyone knows 600,000 words! No one does! Except maybe the ones who wrote the dictionary? She opens it and goes over a few words randomly: anarchist, anarchy, anathema, anatomist, anatomy. One word is especially unfamiliar to her; she reads the entry:

Anathema *noun*

/əˈnæθəmə/

A thing or an idea that you hate because it is the opposite of what you believe.

Racial prejudice is (an) anathema to me.

Interesting, she thinks. She found a new word on the first page she opened in the dictionary. There must be so many more that she doesn't know. As a new fan of words, she felt a little overwhelmed. It is impractical to open the dictionary and read words to learn. "As soon as I move on to a new word, I would forget the previous one!" She sighs in despair and goes back to Don Juan.

The Importance Of Vocabulary

Words constitute the basis of our communication with the people around us and link us to those who have passed on through their writing. Reading and vocabulary go hand in hand, for what you read is a collection of words, after all. Building vocabulary is, in fact, one of those unconstrained skills that we develop continuously throughout our entire lives [1].

An important aspect of being a good reader is to keep building our reading vocabulary. A rich vocabulary will not only help us to comprehend complex texts, and thus become better readers, but also assist us in writing such texts, as well as engaging in eloquent oral communication [2].

As someone who is aiming to become a better reader, you probably read a lot and might encounter a few words that you do not know. But just like Elizabeth, who shared with us a little moment of a stream of her consciousness, you might feel despair with the number of words that you do not know.

What we usually do when encountering an unfamiliar word is either look it up in a dictionary, or the context is comprehensible enough that we can just move on reading as we get a hint of what the sentence means. However, after figuring out the meaning of a word in a particular context, you might find yourself coming across it in another, and may again need help figuring out what it means there. So how can we improve our vocabulary and add more words to our memory bank?

Going Back To Basics

Before touching upon the different approaches to understanding a word, let us start with the very basics. What is vocabulary? In short, it is the knowledge of words [3]; those words that we need in order to understand what we read. The first thing that occurs to us when trying to understand a word is to figure out its synonym to apprehend its meaning.

The editor of *the Oxford English Dictionary*, Sir James Murray, created a diagram in the preface of the dictionary's version of 1884 that illustrates the structure of the relationship between the core words and their diversities or synonyms. The diagram below gives the main framework allowing us to categorize different kinds of words set in a fundamental hierarchical structure of usage, from literary down to slang [4].

If we want to take an illustrated example of Murray's diagram to a certain notion, we would be able to construct a "semantic field" or a number of synonyms for that particular notion. The second diagram illustrates the field of the word "pregnant," giving several synonyms for the word according to the diagram.

*FigureSEQ Figure \ * ARABIC 2 - The Semantic field of the word
"pregnant" [3]
Diagram 2*

Of course, many more terms that would fit perfectly in the diagram can be used. For example, *expecting* can be a little above pregnant; *a bun in the oven* is right before *up the spout* (which is British slang); while *impregnated* – which is used more in writing than in speech – can be used along with *parturient* under the scientific category.

This activity has several values for the knowledge of words [5]:

1. It helps to highlight the synonyms of a particular word, yet defines the different usages of those synonyms.

Although all of the words mentioned above refer to someone who is pregnant, not all can be used interchangeably in every context.

2. It sheds light on the different categories of words, differentiating between scientific, colloquial, and technical terms.

3. The "dialectical" field is important as it depends on the location the word is used. *Knocked up*, for instance, is a strictly American colloquial term.

The Knowledge Of Words

This diagram helps us to figure out the many synonyms of a word or its semantic field, but the knowledge of words contains much more than just what they mean. That knowledge should include the following [6]:

- Phonology – the way a word sounds and how it is pronounced.
- Morphology – the word's structure or the parts that make up the word.
- Grammar – the word's class, form, and function within a sentence.
- Semantics - the meaning of a word that sometimes varies according to context and the way a word is linked to other words.
- Syntax – the way words are arranged, allowing them to form sentences.

We should be aware of all of those details when trying to understand a new word and not just the meaning of that word. This is because the same word can have another meaning in a different context, and we need to rely on much more than mere synonyms to understand what the word refers to.

Let us take an example of a simple word that we can all discern its intended meaning in different contexts. We all know what the word *lost* means, and we can easily understand its connotations in those various contexts that use the word *lost* without pondering about it:

He lost his book.

He was lost.

The Rams lost the Super Bowl.

She lost her mind.

They lost their cool.

He just lost it.

Get lost.

The meaning of *lost* changes in each of those sentences. Since it is the same word, then its phonetic pronunciation and morphology are similar, yet it differs in terms of grammar, semantics, and syntax in every sentence. And we can understand the difference in every sentence. How can we understand new or more difficult words in a similar manner?

It goes without saying that the more one reads, the more vocabulary we are able to develop. This is because readers usually come across many more words than those who do not read, and as they encounter words repeatedly in different contexts, they develop a larger vocabulary [7].

Approaches To Vocabulary Learning

When we want to learn new vocabulary, we mainly refer to two different approaches [8]: direct and indirect learning. Starting from upper elementary grades, we gain new vocabulary through direct teaching (i.e., being told what a word means), learning from context (i.e., indirect learning), or a combination of both.

Direct Learning

During our school years, we all had vocabulary lessons in English classes. This is direct learning, where a teacher gives word lessons, synonym drills, word classifications, definitions, and sentence production exercises. Many studies provide evidence that although such learning approaches are successful to such an extent, there are major doubts that direct teaching of words is the main reason for vocabulary growth in children.

This is probably why we often tend to forget what a word means after we read its definition in the dictionary. Eventually, Elizabeth was somehow right in her despair. It is practically impossible to open up a dictionary, read an unfamiliar word's definition, and consider that we have now learned a new word. The word and its definition are stored in our short-term memory, and consolidation wouldn't occur by simply reading the definition.

Indirect Learning

The second approach to learning new vocabulary occurs indirectly, aka deriving the meaning of a word from context. However, there is little empirical evidence that supports that we achieve learning new words from contextual experiences. This is because it is a little more difficult to measure its effectiveness accurately.

Nevertheless, one study suggests that since school English books require the knowledge of around 88,500 distinct words, it is practically impossible to learn them from direct teaching or dictionary consultation. Thus, the only reasonable argument is that students learn an adequate number of those words through context inference [9].

Building Your Reading Vocabulary

We need to use both direct and indirect approaches to learn new vocabulary as adults. Obviously, we all know how to use a dictionary – which is what direct learning is. Yet, as research suggests, looking up a word in a dictionary or someone telling us what it means doesn't always lead to learning the word. Indirect learning is a fundamental approach that allows us to move the new words from our short-term memory to our long-term one. So how can we successfully deduce meaning from context?

The Context

First, let us understand what is meant by *context*. A context within a given text includes the syntactic, morphological, and discourse information in that text. But there is also a more general context that refers to the reader's background knowledge when processing a text [10]. This background knowledge is an important component of text comprehension [11].

Good readers should always take advantage of what they know when reading. This allows them to create expectations about the kind of vocabulary they would encounter [12]. In an experiment that aimed at monitoring the effect of background knowledge, researchers gave learners some information about the topic of a text prior to reading it. This has assisted the readers in correctly guessing the meaning of many nonsense words within the text [13].

Several studies were conducted to measure the effectiveness of trying to figure out the meaning of a word from context. Good readers were able to guess between 60% and 80% of unknown words within a text [14]. But guessing a word's meaning from context requires a precise strategy to figure out unfamiliar words successfully.

The Procedure

The following procedure can assist readers in making good use of context clues to try and understand a word through an indirect approach. Once a reader is proficient enough in using the clues, the steps below won't be needed to be followed so strictly. For this strategy to work, two presuppositions need to be valid [15]:

1. The reader should easily be able to follow the text they are reading, as in, they should have a good command of most of the vocabulary within the text and have basic comprehension skills.

2. Readers should have a sort of background knowledge about the text.

Both of those conditions will ensure that the reader is able to guess more words from within the text. The main strategy has five different steps [16]:

Step one – Find the unfamiliar word's morphology

This means that you need to try to check the form of the word as a clue to its meaning. Start by dividing it into a prefix, root word, and suffix whenever feasible. For example, the word *preordained* has all three parts: *pre*/ordain /*ed*. This can help you guess what the word means.

Step two – Look at the immediate context of the word and simplify it.

We can simplify the immediate context by looking for a few things in the surrounding text of the unfamiliar word:

1. Answer the question "what does what?" about the word.

2. Take note of any relative clauses or related phrases.

3. Divide the sentence into simpler sentences by removing *and/or*.

4. Check the punctuation for any clues. Is there a quotation mark, use of italics, dashes, or brackets?

Step three – Check the wider context of the word.

After checking the immediate sentence where the unfamiliar word is, we need to look at the wider context and the surrounding sentences. Usually, all sentences in a text have a relationship with the surrounding ones. Such relationships include cause and effect, explanation, detail, contrast, time, and order. We can understand those relationships from adverbs, propositions, and other clues such as the use of *on the contrary, finally, instead, subsequently, firstly, in other words, before,* etc. You can also use reference words within the text such as *it, this, that,* etc.

Step four – Guess the meaning of the unknown word

From the clues you gathered from the first three steps, you should have enough information to allow you to attempt to understand the word and guess its meaning.

Step five - Check if you are right

If you intend to actually learn the new word, you shouldn't only stop at guessing what the word means. You need to make sure that you have correctly guessed it. You can first re-read the sentences or context with the definition or synonym in mind and check if it makes sense within the context. Ultimately, you can refer to the dictionary to make sure that you have understood the word.

You might think: "If I was going to end up using the dictionary, why did I need to go through this strenuous activity of guessing what the word means in the first place?" It is true that trying to figure out what a word means would eventually put your reading activity to a halt for a while, but learning through this indirect approach is much more beneficial than going straight to the dictionary.

Figuring out a word's meaning from the context will effectively help a reader understand how this word is used within a particular context[17]. Recall the several usages of the word *lost* previously mentioned. If one wants to understand how a word is used, they would need much more than a definition or a synonym.

Finally, it is important to try as much as possible to use a new word in different contexts, whether in speech or writing, to ensure that it has become part of your vocabulary bank.

Action Plan

Try to read the first chapter of Thomas Hardy's *The Return of the Native* [18]entitled "A face on which time makes but little impression." Depending on your vocabulary level, you might encounter many or a few unfamiliar words. Try to guess their meaning from the text. The first chapter of the novel is a description of the scenery set in Egdon Heath. You should read the author's preface to gain a little background knowledge about the area being described. Hardy has also provided a map for Egdon Heath, so make use of all such clues to read the chapter and guess the unfamiliar words' meanings from the context following the steps described in this chapter.

Note – If there is a word that you couldn't guess correctly, find what it means from the dictionary. After you do, try to retrace the first three steps even after you have understood its meaning and figure out a way to guess its meaning from the context. If there were any clues that you missed, you'd be able to find them after you know what the word means.

Summary

Part of our journey of becoming better readers and understanding more of what we read is to understand individual words within the text. As Elizabeth has figured, it is mostly useless to try and just open the dictionary and find new words at random. The more we read, the more we encounter new words. And finding the meaning of a word from within a context is the best way to understand it fully and add to our knowledge.

Key Takeaways

Learning a new word should encompass the knowledge of all of the details of the word and not just its meaning because a word can mean different things in different contexts.

The knowledge of words should include its:

- Phonology – the way a word sounds and how it is pronounced.
- Morphology – the word's structure or the parts that make up the word.
- Grammar – the word's class, form, and function within a sentence.
- Semantics - the meaning of a word that sometimes varies according to context and the way a word is linked to other words.
- Syntax – the way words are arranged, allowing them to form sentences.

There are two approaches to learning new vocabulary: Direct learning and indirect learning.

Direct learning is learning what a word means from a dictionary or someone else.

Indirect learning is figuring out the meaning of a word from the context, which includes the syntactic, morphological, and discourse information within that text, as well as the reader's background knowledge.

To guess an unfamiliar word from a text:

- Step 1 – Figure out the word's morphology

- Step 2 – Understand and simplify the immediate context.
- Step 3 – Check the wider context around the word.
- Step 4 – Guess the word's meaning.
- Step 5 – Check if your guess is correct.

9

SPECIALIZED READING TECHNIQUES

CHOOSE THE RIGHT TOOL FOR EVERY TERRAIN -
FROM NOVELS TO SCIENCE

Let's Read

We have already covered the four levels of reading, and have mentioned that the best reading is the one that occurs at the third level, which is analytically. However, not every rule within that level can apply to every book. It would be very difficult, for instance, to figure out the most important words, sentences, and propositions of an author when you are reading a story. There is no point in doing so.

Let us take the list of books below:

Arms and the Man by George Bernard Shaw

Beyond Good and Evil by Friedrich Nietzsche

The Math of Life and Death: 7 Mathematical Principles That Shape Our Lives by Kit Yates

Steve Jobs by Walter Isaacson

The Ten Basic Principles of Good Parenting by Laurence D. Steinberg

Shakespeare's Sonnets & Poems by William Shakespeare

A Brief History in Time by Stephen Hawking

The American Civil War, 1861 – 1865 by Reid Mitchell

The Wretched of the Earth by Frantz Fanon

1984 by George Orwell

Each book on this list, as is the case with every book, has a different purpose. Whether or not you've encountered one of those books before, you should know that every one of them can be read analytically, with slight differences in the rules mentioned in chapter 5. In this chapter, we will go over those differences by looking at various types of books, and how to read each analytically.

Analytical Questions

There were many rules for analytical reading, all of which tend to answer four main questions:

1. What is the book about? What is the main theme of the book? And how did the author develop it?
2. What are the main ideas and arguments that the author used to relay the message?
3. Is what this book is saying true or not?
4. What is the significance of the information within this book?

If we want to read a book well, we first need to understand it, and then be able to criticize it. For every kind of book, there is a different way of doing so. For instance, we cannot read a cookbook the same way we read a novel or a chemistry book. However, in all cases, we can ultimately answer the four questions of analytical reading. So how do we do that for different kinds of books?

Changing Your Mind

Our aim in this book is to help you read better by giving you a set of rules and laying down some principles about how to read better. This kind of book falls into the expository category. They are books that tend to inform and explain to a reader something about a specific topic [1].

Expository books are mainly divided into two different categories: practical and theoretical books [2]. They both aim to persuade the reader by defining a certain problem and providing a solution for that problem. Their ultimate objective is to convince the reader that the solution they provide is the best. The difference between the two kinds of expository books is that practical books have rules that solve the problem, while theoretical books set out the underlying principles of the solution.

Practical books do not solve the problem but call for action by the reader. For example, the book you are now reading is a practical book. The problem is to read books better. You can read it from cover to cover, but the problem wouldn't be solved without action on your part, without you trying to apply the rules stated within the book to become a better reader. The same goes for reading a cookbook, for instance. If you do use the recipe to create a dish, the "problem" won't be solved.

In contrast, a theoretical book lays out a problem and solves it within the book. There is no action required from the part of the reader, except maybe some mental activity, when considering the problem and the solution laid out. *Capital: Critique of Political Economy* written by Karl Marx is an example of a theoretical book. Marx laid out his theory about capitalism, attempted to show its contradictions, and criticized economic theory, which he believed was faulty at its core [3]. Obviously, no action is required after reading *Capital*, but Marx attempted to persuade readers of his theories about capitalism.

Of course, such a distinction between expository books is not absolute. Sometimes a book might have both principles and rules at the same time. But it is more or less easy to identify a practical book from a theoretical one. Generally speaking, the nature of the problem within the book should lead you to know what kind of expository book it is. A practical book is usually about human behavior, and the author would suggest a way in which humans can somehow improve in that particular field.

Now that we understand the difference between the two kinds of expository books, let us go over some details of how to read each one analytically.

Practical Books

All practical books have rules, maxims, or a general direction for the reader to follow. Of course, we need to answer the first two questions of analytical reading. We need to find what the main topic is about, and the objectives or purpose for writing the book. This will help readers to understand and criticize it properly.

When it comes to the following steps of analytical reading, the main propositions that you need to look for when reading a practical book are the rules that the author lays out. The arguments supporting his propositions should be the author's explanation for the suggested rules. The author should attempt to persuade you as to why following such rules will help you to achieve the book's objective.

After you find the objectives, discern the rules the author suggests, and the arguments that support the suggestions, you can start criticizing the book. Depending on the book you're reading, the author's recommendations could be thorough, yet you might not agree with the methodology. If you think analytically and intelligently when reading a practical book, you might agree with the author, follow their rules, and take action, or simply not agree and state why or how they haven't convinced you.

Theoretical Book

A theoretical book will usually lay out principles from which rules can be generated. But the main focus of a theoretical book is the theory itself, which is usually a set of propositions laid out by the author. The arguments will be an attempt to prove those propositions that make up the theory.

An example of a theory is Charles Darwin's theory of evolution laid out in his book *On the Origin of Species*. Darwin's main proposition was that individuals with specific traits that allow them to adapt to the environment would survive, while others would perish. This accounts for what he termed "natural selection." Throughout his book, he made arguments based on the observations he noted across different species. Even though Darwin had no idea about genetics, which wasn't available during his lifetime, future research made by geneticists gave additional evidence about Darwin's natural selection theory [4].

This is an important aspect to remember about theory. It is accumulative, and many people can add to the theory, refute it altogether, or argue against it - even years after the book was published. For instance, after almost a century from when Marx wrote *Capital* (written in 1867), Milton Friedman refuted Marx's theory in *Capitalism and Freedom* (written in 1962). Friedman, in contrast, celebrated capitalism and argued that all society needs is unrestrained and free markets [5].

When a reader wants to agree or disagree with a theory, they should relate their arguments to what the author is saying, to their theory, and the reasoning behind it. As with any book you read, you are free to agree or disagree, but you need to develop your arguments about why you do or don't based on what's in the book you are criticizing.

On another note, if you have noticed, Darwin created the term "natural selection." Figuring out the author's terms in theoretical books is a very crucial step in reading analytically. So an analytical reader needs to understand the theory, the key terms laid out by the author, and the arguments made to prove that theory before judging a theoretical book.

Finally, it is important in the case of theoretical books to understand a little background about the author. One cannot fully understand *The Communist Manifesto* without understanding the background of the lives of its authors – Friedrich Engels and Karl Marx – how they lived, and what they were trying to do by laying out the theories in the book. Whether the theories that you read in books are relevant today or not goes back to the judgment that you make.

Living In A Different World

The second category is fiction books. A fiction book, whether a novel, story, or play, creates stories, sets them in new worlds, and takes you, the reader, into that world. The primary objective of fiction is to please the reader. And although it is much easier to please a reader than persuade them with an idea, concept, or solution for a problem, it is much more difficult for the reader to say why they were pleased – or displeased.

This is because beauty is much harder to analyze than truth.

The difference between expository books and fiction is that the first needs to have everything clearly laid out to persuade the reader of what they are proposing. Yet with fiction, what can be implied and what lies between the lines is as important as what is being said, if not more. An analytical reader might understand or conclude something from a story that does not exist within the book's pages.

An analytical reading entices the reader to find the terms, propositions, and arguments in a book. But with fiction, finding terms, propositions, and arguments isn't always clear-cut. Instead, we need to look at the characters, their thoughts, their feelings, as well as the action that happens [6]. So how do we go about reading a fiction book analytically?

<u>Novels Or Short Stories</u>

Whether long or short, a story should be read as quickly as possible from cover to cover [7]. Readers should immerse themselves within that new and different world, live and feel with the characters, and not stop until the very end of the story. Once you do, you will be able to answer the first analytical question of what the book is about. You will be able to understand the plot, what happened, and relate to the characters created in the book.

The German novelist Gustav Freytag pinpointed the five

stages a plot should go through within a good storyline. The below figure represents those five stages [8]:

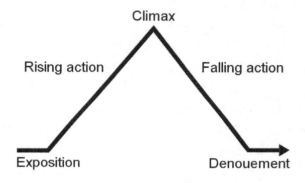

Your first task as an analytical reader is to be able to discern this plot. How did the story start (exposition), what happened [rising action], what was the problem (climax), how was it solved (falling action), and how did it end (denouement)? Many stories, however, have many more details and much more complicated plots than would fit into one diagram. But you need to be able to discern that main storyline and understand what it is about and what happened.

Once you've answered the first analytical question, you can focus on the terms of the book. Those are its characters, which you need to get to know, and the incidents that happened, which you should be able to sort out. The propositions within a fiction book are the setting, the background, and the world the characters live in. So what an analytical reader should do is immerse themselves fully in that world, make it their home while reading, and live there with the characters [9].

As you get to know the plot and what happened, understand the characters, how they evolved, and live with them in their fictional world, you will be able to close the book and think. You will be able to judge the action of the characters, you will be able to feel if what happened was just or unjust, and you will be able to know why you were pleased or displeased with the outcome, and the book as a whole.

Many stories are there to make you think for hours, if not days, after you close the book. *Beloved* by Toni Morrison is basically a ghost story. Yet the depth that one finds within its pages, and its complex and rich narrative will make the novel's haunting become the reader's "historical consciousness" [10]. The narrative around that ghost story depicts the lasting and harrowing effects of slavery. An analytical reader would discern the many psychological, historical, and cultural connotations in the novel. They should understand what lies between the lines, think through what happens, and discern why they liked or disliked what they read.

Plays

A play is similar to a novel as it also tells a story. Yet the reader needs to actively create the background and setting about which a written play has few details. The main difference between reading a novel and a play is that a play is not meant to be read in the first place; it is meant to be watched. So if you have the opportunity to see a play that you'd like to read, by all means, do so.

Plays were written to be performed by actors. The director, as well as the actors, have as much say in how the emotions are laid out as much as the play's author does [11]. But generally speaking, the same terms and conditions that apply to novels are applied to plays, written and performed. You need to understand the plot, the characters, the setting, read between the lines, and make a judgment about what you've read or seen.

Poems

Like all fiction books, a poem needs to be read from start to end continuously, even if the reader feels they do not understand. It needs to be read in its entirety in order to grasp its essence.

After finishing that first reading, it is recommended for the reader to read it again out loud. What makes a poem stand out is its rhythm and rhymes; it is what gives a poem its beauty. And this beauty is what we look for, in contrast with the truth that we look for in expository books.

Part of a poem's beauty is to feel it resonate aloud. Your ears are part of the reading process of a poem. So read the poem again out loud. After this second reading, you will be able to discern the keywords. They would simply stand out while saying them. This is the magic of poetry. Once you find those words, you start asking yourself, why does this word stand out? Is it the rhythm? The rhyme? A sort of repetition that takes place? This is where the art of the poet shines.

To read a good poem is to share the feelings that the poet wanted to share. Experience what they are saying, and the better the poem, the more immersed in that feeling you would be. Read it again, and after a few readings, you can start to look for any unknown words to understand – either through context or from a dictionary. And then read again. What you ask of a poem is more rhetorical questions rather than logical ones [12]. And what you discern from a poem can be as personal and as free as you would want it to be.

Matthew Arnold, one of the most influential Victorian critics and poets, considered poetry as the way to interpret life. He even stated that it would surpass philosophy and science as it is the one medium of expression that truly evokes emotions [13]. Try to find the hidden beauty within the poems that you read and re-read. You will be able to learn more about it every time you go back and read it again [14].

Going Back in Time

Another category is history books. They mostly also do tell stories, yet those stories are real; they happened to some people, somewhere, at some point in time. When we read history books, we need to understand the fact that they are not fiction. This is a real story, that might have altered the course of history at some point, and thus we will need to discern the truth from them.

All that remains of history is evidence from written material or crumbling physical locations, as well as testimonies of people who are long gone. Yet, as a good analytical reader with a history book in front of you, you need to be able to judge whether or not the historian who wrote this book is stating accurate facts. And since many historical events tend to be distorted and the details are lost along the way, a good reader needs to read more than one account of the period or event in order to understand it fully [15].

A history book aims to discover or determine what happened, why it happened, and what led the people at the time to act the way they did [16]. Depending on the author, the Crusades, for instance, were either an attempt to defend Christians and the Christian Holy sites or were an aggressive invasion of the Middle East by Europe. An analytical reader needs to read history from different viewpoints before criticizing or taking a stance.

History Books

Although history books tell more of a story, they must still be read like expository books. And thus, similar questions should apply. However, the questions asked as well as their answers should be a little different. Regarding the first analytical question, we need to know what subject the history book is discussing, and what era, period, or event they are talking about in the book.

Secondly, we need to understand how the historian chose to tell the story. We need to find out how their book is organized. Did they divide it thematically or chronologically? A good indication would be to look at the table of contents and do a quick inspectional reading of the book. This will allow the reader to know where the historian puts emphasis when telling that story, allowing us to understand them better.

When we intend to criticize a history book, we first need to find out if the author interpreted the sources correctly. This can be felt in many cases with old historians who tend to ignore economic discussions when trying to talk about an event in the past. Sometimes, we might find that the author didn't use the sources correctly. They might be uninformed about a certain detail that we have read in another book. This is why reading several books about a historical event or period is necessary for a true analytical reading of history.

When it comes to the last question of analytical reading, we must consider the effects of what history has on our current lives. More often than not, history tells us the tales of the past, so maybe we can change the status of things in the present. What's important about reading history correctly, is that those things that have happened can either happen again, or be avoided altogether [17]. And we can only learn from history when we read about it properly.

Biographies And Autobiographies

Biographies and autobiographies are also part of history, talking about a single person's life. And accordingly, they have the same issues as history books. The questions about biographies start by inquiring why the author wrote the book, and what are the criteria of truth in the book.

You must, however, know the different kinds of biographies in order to differentiate between them. First, there are definitive biographies that are intended to be exhaustive and complete scholarly works talking about the life of someone who is very important and worthy of such a biography. Exhaustive biographies are usually written after the person's death, and usually follow the publication of several other non-definitive biographies that aren't as extensive.

The other type of biography is authorized biographies, which are written by a friend or a family member of someone important. Those writers are usually commissioned to write the biography and are very careful in what they depict within the book to make the person appear in the best possible light. Those biographies need to be approached with caution as they might be biased. They are better taken into account when the reader is aware that this is how this person's family or friend saw them.

And, of course, there remain autobiographies that are especially problematic in their own right. First, they are written about a life story that is yet to be completed. Secondly, it is very difficult indeed to know and understand one's own life. But some are brilliantly written, and it is very interesting to see how some people describe their own lives. *The Autobiography of Benjamin Franklin* and *The Diary of Anne Frank* are a couple of good examples.

On a final note, if you are interested about a person in history, as a good reader, you should also read as many biographies (including autobiographies if one is written) as you can to get to know that person fully [18]. Biographies should be read as part of history, understand what happened and why, and argue with the author. The last question you can ponder is, what of it? Depending on the person you are reading about - who we expect should be interesting enough to have biographies written about them - they could be someone who is inspiring. You can learn something about your own life that you still need to lead when hearing a story about someone else's.

<u>Current Events</u>

Another type of history is the stories that are currently occurring around us. Maybe it is an event that happened a few years back, or even last week. This can encompass books about major events that affected our world, like the events of 9/11, for example, or a newspaper that is talking about the events that happened yesterday.

Reporters' main job is to report the news of what is happening in the world in an unbiased way. They usually aim at transferring the truth they are witnessing as objectively as possible. However, especially after the surge of the phenomena of "fake news," one must start to consider reading the daily news analytically as well.

In 2005, a study was published that measured the bias of the major US media outlets and concluded that there was a strong liberal bias in almost all major media outlets. This is most probably the case because news producers prefer to cater to certain kinds of consumers, which would, in turn, attract more advertisers to use their outlets [19]. Regardless of your political position, a good reader is a truth seeker in whatever they read. So we need to be aware of biases when reading or even watching any current news.

Nowadays, things are getting even more complicated with everyone having a platform to say what they think and believe is true. So we end up hearing loads of different viewpoints from everyone. An analytical reader interested in getting to know the truth about any event must also read and look for different sources discussing the topic. Just like reading about any historical event, our current events are stories that are yet to be completed. Read analytically anything you come across, and understand it from different viewpoints before judging and giving your own opinion.

The Science World

In today's world, unless you are specialized in a certain field, we rarely tend to go near any specialized books of science. This is understandable because, starting in the twentieth century, the divisions in the various disciplines have separated people in academia. A physicist rarely reads a medical book, and a chemist is no longer interested in reading about mathematics. However, before the divisions of institutions, authors like Sir Isaac Newton and the astronomer Galileo Galilei wrote for the public [20].

In fact, the term "discipline" is originally a Roman term "disciplina" that applied to only a few professions, such as medicine and law, which required learning specialized information about a topic. Every educated person reads everything else as part of their knowledge. In the twentieth century, disciplines as we know them started to develop. What was known as "natural philosophy" at the time was divided into new categories: physics, mathematics, and chemistry; social sciences were also segmented into anthropology and political economy, out of the latter were formed political science and economics, and then later we got history, sociology, and psychology.

All universities started to get organized around the different disciplines [21]. Every group of people from every discipline started to have their own terms and methodologies. And the experts in a field tend to write to other experts in that same field today. Of course, this method has advantages, as it serves science best by helping it advance more quickly. An expert can recognize a problem from another's research or theory, and find a solution. Yet one of the problems is that we, the public, the ones who aim to read and understand better, who aren't experts in a certain field, are left out [22].

Nevertheless, today, we have interdisciplinary studies that tend to challenge this division, reunite the disciplines, and anchor their approaches to science. Academia is again trying to tighten the gaps between the disciplines. And as good readers, we need to learn, at the very least, how to read science even if it isn't our "specialty."

The Scientific Method

Prior to reading any scientific book or research, we first need to understand the scientific method used in scientific discourse. The scientific method is a systematic way of allowing us to learn about the world and answer the questions that the scientist is inquiring about. It mainly involves six steps [23]:

Step 1 – Asking a question that would define the problem and guide the research in question. This step can include making certain observations about the subject matter.

Step 2 – Background research. No good science discourse is complete without looking extensively at previous research that tried to solve the problem. If the question was asked before and a solution was presented, then the current research based on that question isn't worth the effort.

Step 3 – Proposing a hypothesis which is usually an educated guess about what the scientist or researcher is assuming the results would be.

Step 4 – Designing and performing an experiment or a set of experiments to answer the main question(s). The experiments can differ between disciplines. A psychologist can perform a social experiment while a chemist's experiment is in a lab.

Step 5 – Making observations and analyzing the data. Usually, the data would be presented in the form of a graph or a chart.

Step 6 – Conclude whether the hypothesis posed is accepted or rejected. An experiment has no right or wrong, the results need to be laid out objectively, and the conclusion given should be a logical explanation of the results.

Even if you do not need to do research or are unrelated to any scientific discipline, a good reader should know how we come up with science. Whenever you are interested in a topic, we all rely on scientific results to support our viewpoints. The data or results you rely upon come from a defined methodology, and a good reader should be able to discern good research with reasonable results from the ones that aren't.

The Abstract In Mathematics

The field of mathematics is a different kind of science that doesn't rely on observations and experiments but has its own language, symbols, and methods. Whether you liked the subject of math back in school or hated it, you should already know that it is included in everything in life. All other sciences need math to prove their theories and complete their research. But the difficulty for the average reader attempting to understand math is its abstract nature that eludes the efforts of the mental abilities of readers [24].

Math has its own language indeed, and just like trying to learn a new language, one needs to start at the elementary level. We need to understand what certain symbols and the relationships between those symbols mean to understand [25].

You might start thinking at this moment, why would I need to learn to read math? Mainly, because math is the foundation of how we think about natural phenomena. So how can we understand math and think differently about it?

First, we need to understand the abstract notion that is math. Math deals with ideas and properties that are applicable to things just because they exist, and those properties apply regardless of how we feel about them. When we think about math, an average person would think about two plus two equals four, for example. This is arithmetic, and it applies to everything: sounds, tastes, oranges, angels, the bones in the body, and the ideas in the mind. Every two and two makes four.

Secondly, the importance of math as a science is that its abstractness lies at the core of scientific thought. Everything around us has interconnections. We see lightning in the sky, we know thunder will follow; and we know that if I am holding a ball and let go of it, it will fall to the ground. All scientific progress is based on observations of the order of the world we live in.

Scientific thought is to see what is general, particular, and transitory. And everything we observe is governed by laws that science tries to uncover. Those laws, like the law of gravity, need to be laid out universally.

Even though my sensations differ from yours, we both live in the same world that is governed by those same laws regardless of how we individually feel about them. Those laws, devoid of any personal feelings or experiences, are the properties of things; those laws are the abstract mathematical ideas describing the order of the world we live in [26].

Any reader who intends to expand their horizons beyond their own experiences and their own thoughts need basic knowledge of mathematics [27]. Reading and understanding mathematics, even at the elementary level, is our way to understand the laws of the world and the order of things around us. It is the basis of every other science and the basis of how our world functions. So when reading math, aim to understand the language at the elementary level prior to moving forward.

Questioning The World

The last group of books we will go over is those of philosophy. Just like science in the modern days, philosophers have their own terms and usually tend to write to other philosophers [28]. In contrast with science, which looks at life and tries to explain it, the aim of philosophy is to ask questions about life, existence, and being human, amongst many more. When you are face to face with a philosophical book, the first thing you need to uncover is the question(s) the author is trying to answer.

You have to keep in mind that philosophy is just like science in the modern days. Every new philosophical book continues to answer previously asked questions and add to them. It is a continuous story that started with the first philosophical questions the oldest human being has ever asked (Why do we exist? What is our purpose? What is good and what is evil? These are just a few general examples).

So we need to read additional books that relate to the question(s) asked, aiming at retrieving older books about the topic. This will help us understand the concepts that current philosophers are basing their new concepts on. Otherwise, we can make use of a philosophy dictionary to understand the terms the author uses, which every knowledgeable person about philosophy should know.

Reading Philosophy

As mentioned earlier, first, we need to know the questions the philosopher is asking. They might be stated explicitly or implicitly within the text; either way, we need to discern those questions [29].

Secondly, we need to find the author's definitions of terms. Vocabulary can vary greatly from author to author, so coming to terms with the author is a crucial step in reading philosophical books. If you've ever come across the Stanford Encyclopedia of Philosophy, you notice that they not only define every term but also explain the context in which a certain author uses it. For instance, *Game Theory* is "the study of interdependent choice and action" and includes "the study of strategic decision making." On the other hand, you will find another entry for *Game Theory*, which is used by economists, biologists, and social scientists, and has a mathematical formulation to it.

After finding the questions and understanding the definitions of the main keywords or terms the author uses, we need to find the author's arguments. These include the premise and conclusion, the objections to those conclusions, and the solutions the author offers to those objections, along with their reasoning behind them.

Another important aspect of most philosophical discourses is the use of examples, which the analytical reader should also find. Philosophers use examples to clarify their points [30]. It would help us in understanding the concepts or arguments they are proposing.

Finally, once you feel you understand the questions posed, the arguments, conclusions, objections, and solutions, along with the examples, you can start by contesting with the author's ideas. Understanding philosophy is a strenuous mental activity, but it is worthwhile. And discussing philosophy with someone or hypothetically with the author of a book is one of the most fulfilling activities we can have as good readers.

Theology

Theology examines the existence of God or the creator of everything. There are two kinds of theological books. The first is natural theology, which is part of philosophy [31]. Natural theology attempts to argue the existence of a creator by observing natural facts. As a philosophical branch, it uses all human faculties, including reason, introspection, and our senses to investigate theological issues [32].

The second kind of theology is dogmatic theology, which is not considered part of philosophy. It mainly relies on articles of faith and depends on the dogmas and the authority of the religion that proclaims them [33]. All scripture books, including the Torah, the Bible, and the Quran, are the basis of the principles of dogmatic theology of the Abrahamic religions.

Obviously, reading a natural theology book is read the same way a philosophy book is. However, when attempting to read dogmatic theological books you need to keep in mind that it is based primarily on faith. If you are not of faith and want to read a dogmatic theology book, you can read it just as you read a math book, treating the dogmas just as you'd treat mathematical assumptions. For the faithful, faith is not a matter of opinion; it is a form of knowledge.

The first mistake a reader makes when attempting to read and understand dogmatic theology is that they refuse to accept that the articles of faith are the author's principles.

Those articles and dogmas are not negotiable, and the author's writing is based upon that. So even if temporarily, an analytical reader needs to read while keeping in mind that the articles of faith are true.

This does not mean that the arguments the author proposes, their line of reasoning, and their conclusions are also dogmatic. In fact, this is where an analytical reader can intervene and argue with the author. The reason that the author makes is based on principles that are not to be refuted, but an analytical reader can either accept the author's line of reasoning and agree with their conclusions, or find it defective.

If you were a believer, you would be able to argue with the author's line of reasoning about certain ideas that do not usually conflict with your faith, albeit being based on it. But a non-believer should start by accepting that the first principles and dogmas are true in order to understand and criticize the book [34]. It would be unproductive to argue with a theologian if you both do not have the same starting point, which is faith.

Action Plan

An analytical reader first needs to be able to read a book is identify what kind of book it is. Go back to the list of books in this chapter's introduction and try to determine what kind of book each one is. If you are unfamiliar with an author or a certain entry, it is a good idea to do preliminary research about it and use your critical and analytical skills to understand what each one is about. Through your research, you might be able to discern the kind of book it is, what it is about, and maybe the main questions that the author asks within each book. If you find any book of interest, by all means, read it, analytically.

Summary

Reading books analytically involves a set of rules that slightly differ from one kind of book to the other. This chapter attempted to define those differences and guide the analytical reader to the kinds of books available as well as the various ways each book can be read. Of course, there are many additional details for reading each kind of book, but the above merely provides general guidance on how each kind is organized and the way an analytical reader needs to think when faced with a certain book in order to read and understand it better.

<u>Key Takeaways</u>

- There are different kinds of books, and each kind is read and understood differently.
- We need to understand the kind of book and why it is written in order to read it analytically.
- Expository books are divided into practical and theoretical books. They aim to persuade the reader with their theory or practical solution to a problem.

- Fiction books are mainly stories in which readers need to immerse themselves to understand them fully. They aim at pleasing the reader and a good reader should understand why they were or were not pleased.
- History, biographies, and news are real stories that attempt to recount the facts that happened. They aim to inform the reader of what happened or is happening, and our role is to discern the truth from them.
- Scientific books aim to understand the world we live in and have a systematic methodology that needs to be followed to come up with a conclusion about how the world functions. They are based on observations and experiments. Mathematics lays down the laws and principles of our world. It is an abstract field that discerns those laws that govern all other scientific fields as well as the world we live in.
- Philosophical books question the world and our existence within that world. They are one of the most difficult books to read and understand. They require the most strenuous, yet fulfilling mental activity.

10

EVALUATE YOUR READING PROGRESS
PRACTICAL TESTS THAT CAN HELP ASSESS YOUR READING SKILLS

This whole book would be useless if you do not start reading actively and critically. So let us start by making use of it with a few reading exercises that would launch the progress of your reading skills.

Learning To Read

As a good reader, you already know how to read English properly and easily. If we want to understand how reading at the elementary level occurs, we need to go back to the basics of deciphering the letters, words, and sentences. One exercise you can do to appreciate your capacity in the mastery of English, is to try and read Middle English.

A great example is the well-known story of King Arthur and the Knights of the Round Table. In 1485, Thomas

Malory wrote the original story entitled *Le Morte D'Arthur*. The language used within the book is known as Middle English, which might appear as a foreign language once you first encounter it, yet it still is English.

Attempting to read those classical books in the original way they were written is a great exercise in mental reading activity, in which you discern the letters and the words. Before reading, let us go over a few principles to follow when reading Middle English [1]:

1. Middle English authors wrote the way they spoke. There was no consistency in the way words were written at the time, and one might find several differences in spelling. Knowing this, you should read Middle English phonetically and be flexible when pronouncing the vowels.

2. Most of the literature from Middle English was written to be read out loud to an audience. All texts are more comprehensible when heard than when viewed. So read the text out loud. For instance, you would encounter in the text below the words *lodgyng, whan, broder, and chircheyard.* They would first look weird but if you attempt reading them aloud phonetically, they would easily be recognized as *lodging, when, brother, and churchyard.*

3. All letters are pronounced. Middle English has no silent letters in the words and every letter is pronounced, even the *e* at the end, which is usually pronounced like an *a* in *about.* (An example is the word *younge* which is pronounced *younga*).

4. Few Middle English authors wrote abstractly. They told comprehensible stories. So if you are faced with an illogical sentence, try to simplify it and think logically about it. The sentence *"he was the hendest man olive"* has nothing to do with edible olives. It would make more sense that the writer used *o* instead of *a* and the word originally refers to *alive*.

Now that we have the basic principles of reading Middle English, let us try to take a part of *Le Morte D'Arthur* [2]. This is the part of the story that occurs after the king has died and everyone is seeking a new king to crown. Merlin advises the archbishops that whoever pulls the sword from the stone in the churchyard after the mass is completed on Christmas will be king. The passage below is about the moment when the young Arthur takes the sword out of the stone, and is consequently chosen to be king.

Reading the below part will give you the sense of the magic of understanding words that, at first look, appears incomprehensible. It is the magic of learning to read as a child. It is okay if you encounter words you do not understand, read it all at first, and remember to read it phonetically and aloud, as it would be much more understandable.

The setting: It was New Year's Day, after the service, and all the barons had gone out to the fields to joust and tourney.

(1) vpon newe yeersday the barons lete maake a Iustes and a tournement

(2) that alle kny3tes shat wold Iuste or tourneye there my3t playe

(3) & all this was ordeyned for to kepe the lordes to gyders & the comyns

(4) For the Archebisshop trusted

(5) that god wold make hym knowe

(6) that shold wynne the swerd

(7) So vpon newe yeresday whan

(8) the seruyce was done the barons rode vnto the feld

(10) some to Iuste & som to torney

(11) & so it happed that syre Ector that had grete lyuelode aboute london rode vnto the Iustes

(12) & with hym rode syr kaynus his sone & yong Arthur that was hys nourisshed broder

(13) & syr kay was made kny3t at al halowmas afore

(14) So as they rode to ye Iustes ward

(15) sir kay lost his swerd for he had lefte it at his faders lodgyng

(16) & so he prayd yong Arthur for to ryde for his swerd

(17) I wyll wel said Arthur

(18) & rode fast after ye swerd

(19) & whan he cam home

(20) the lady & al were out to see the Ioustyng

(21) thenne was Arthur wroth & saide to hym self

(22) I will ryde to the chircheyard

(23) & take the swerd with me that stycketh in the stone

(24) for my broder sir kay shal not be without a swerd this day

(25) so whan he cam to the chircheyard sir Arthur aliȝt & tayed his hors to the style

(26) & so he wente to the tent

(27) & found no knyȝtes there

(28) for they were atte Iustyng & so he handled the swerd by the handels

(29) and liȝtly & fiersly pulled it out of the stone

(30) & took his hors & rode his way vntyll he came to his broder sir kay

(31) & delyuerd hym the swerd

(32) & as sone as sir kay saw the swerd he wist wel it was the swerd of the stone

(33) & so he rode to his fader syr Ector & said sire loo here is the swerd of the stone

(34) wherfor I must be kyng of thys land

(35) when syre Ector beheld the swerd

(36) he retorned ageyne & cam to the chirche

(37) & there they aliȝte al thre & wente in to the chirche

(38) And anon he made sir kay swere vpon a book

(39) How he came to that swerd

(40) Syr said sir kay by my broder Arthur for he brought it to me

(41) how gate ye this swerd said sir Ector to Arthur

(42) sir I will telle you when I cam home for my broders swerd

(43) I fond no body at home to delyuer me his swerd

(44) And so I thought my broder syr kay shold not be swerdles

(45) & so I cam hyder egerly & pulled it out of the stone withoute ony payn found

(46) ye ony knyȝtes about this swerd seid sir ector

(47) Nay said Arthur

(48) Now said sir Ector to Arthur I vnderstāde

(49) ye must be kynge of this land

(50) wherfore I

(51) sayd Arthur and for what cause

(52) Sire saide Ector

(53) for god wille haue hit soo for ther shold neuer man haue drawen oute this swerde

(54) but he that shal be rightwys kyng of this land

(55) Now lete me see whether ye can putte the swerd ther as it was

(56) and pulle hit oute ageyne

(57) that is no maystry said Arthur

(58) and soo he put it in the stone

(59) wherwith alle Sir Ector assayed to pulle oute the swerd and faylled.

Below is a Modern English translation of this excerpt [3]:

Upon New Year's Day, when the service was done, the barons rode unto the field, some to joust and some to tourney. It happened that Sir Ector, that had great livelihood about London, rode unto the jousts, and with him rode Sir Kay his son, and young Arthur that was his nourished brother. Sir Kay was made knight at All Hallowmass afore. So as they rode to the jousts-ward, Sir Kay lost his sword, for he had left it at his father's lodging. So he prayed young Arthur for to ride for his sword.

"I will well," said Arthur, and rode fast after the sword. When he came home, the lady and all were out to see the jousting. Then was Arthur wroth, and said to himself, "I will ride to the churchyard, and take the sword with me that sticketh in the stone, for my brother

Sir Kay shall not be without a sword this day." So when he came to the churchyard, Sir Arthur alighted and tied his horse to the stile. He went to the tent, and found no knights there, for they were at the jousting. And so he handled the sword by the handles, and lightly and fiercely pulled it out of the stone. He then took his horse and rode his way until he came to his brother Sir Kay, and delivered him the sword.

As soon as Sir Kay saw the sword, he wist well it was the sword of the stone. So he rode to his father Sir Ector, and said: "Sir, lo here is the sword of the stone, wherefore I must be king of this land." When Sir Ector beheld the sword, he returned again and came to the church, and there they alighted all three, and went into the church. And anon he made Sir Kay swear upon a book how he came to that sword.

"Sir," said Sir Kay, "by my brother Arthur, for he brought it to me."

"How gat ye this sword?" said Sir Ector to Arthur.

"Sir, I will tell you. When I came home for my brother's sword, I found nobody at home to deliver me his sword; and so I thought my brother Sir Kay should not be swordless, and so I came hither eagerly and pulled it out of the stone without any pain."

"Found ye any knights about this sword?" said Sir Ector.

"Nay," said Arthur.

"Now," said Sir Ector to Arthur, "I understand ye must be king of this land."

"Wherefore I," said Arthur, "and for what cause?"

"Sir," said Ector, *"for God will have it so; for there should never man have drawn out this sword, but he that shall be rightwise king of this land. Now let me see whether ye can put the sword there as it was, and pull it out again."*

"That is no mastery," said Arthur. *And so he put it in the stone; wherewithal Sir Ector assayed to pull out the sword and failed.*

After reading the explanation, try to read again (aloud) the original version above.

Discovering A Book

In today's digital world, there are two kinds of people: those with an online business, who heavily rely on digital marketing to sell their services or products, and the consumers, who are the target of digital marketing. Regardless of which group you belong to, digital marketing is a big part of our lives, whether or not we like it. And it only makes sense that we try to understand it.

Let us get a quick idea about it by inspecting the book *Digital and Social Media Marketing: A Results-Driven Approach.* Through the limited preview from Google books, try to read it at the inspectional level and attempt to assess whether it would be useful to you to read thoroughly. After all, inspectional reading helps you to make up your mind if reading a certain book is worthwhile your time or not.

Go back to <u>Chapter 5</u> and re-read the steps of inspectional reading to make the best use of the limited pages you can access through Google books. If you are not interested in this topic, you can, of course, choose any other book you would like to inspect and apply the steps of inspectional reading. Once you master the step, you will use it unconsciously whenever you are in a library or shopping for books.

Reading Well

This is the time for you to read analytically. It will take time and effort, but will ultimately be the most fulfilling reading experience. We will not impose on you a choice of book to read analytically as this all goes back to your taste. However, since you have nearly finished reading this book, let us try to suggest a few ideas that would determine how well you understood the essence of reading analytically:

- Go over the table of contents of this book again and try to remember everything you have read.
- Read the summaries and key takeaways of each chapter to refresh your memory.
- Now that you know how to read and understand a book better, how would you have read this book differently? What would you change if you wanted to read it analytically?
- Since you've already read the book as a first reading, try to read it again analytically. Do you agree with the concepts within and its chosen

methodology? Do you agree or disagree with the author generally, and why?

The Most Rewarding Activity

Once you are comfortable enough with reading analytically, let us try reading syntopically. As we have mentioned in the previous chapter, many topics are worth reading several books about, like history or philosophy. The first thing you want to define is a subject that interests you enough to read several books on it.

Rather than providing a list of books, here are a few suggestions of general topics. This is because part of the delight of reading syntopically is the reader's research to find the books they think are worthy of reading about the topic. The list of topics below is a mere suggestion, of course, and it all goes back to the reader's interests.

Idea 1 - You can pick any historical event that interests you. Maybe you are interested to learn more about the US Civil war, the cold war, or the rise and fall of the Roman Empire. Or perhaps you are more interested in more recent history, like the conflict in the Middle East or the Vietnam war.

Idea 2 - If you are more into human nature than events, maybe you'd be interested in delving deeper into psychological topics. The idea of insanity and madness is a fascinating search that would lead you to learn about the psychological disorders psychologists were able to differentiate. Maybe you are personally interested in specific psychological disorders like narcissism or depression. Do not stop at getting basic knowledge about the symptoms. Look for books that discuss the topic of interest in detail, try to understand how it evolved, and what led psychologists to the diagnosis of today.

Idea 3 - Maybe you are more interested in social life, so a good topic in anthropology might interest you more. If you are affected by racism, many books discuss the mystery that is the color of the skin. This could lead you to scientific books in biology or take you toward sociological discourses. If you are interested in feminism you can start digging and reading about certain concepts about the topic and researching matriarchal societies.

Idea 4 - Perhaps you would like to try a more philosophical idea. You might be interested in the ethics and morality prevalent in our modern world and the reasoning behind them. If so, utilitarianism is a good place to start.

Honestly, the list of topic suggestions can go on and on. It would encompass business, science, sociology, and technology like nanotechnology and Artificial Intelligence. The sky is the limit.

If you have noticed, even when we were trying to single out a certain field to narrow down a topic, every topic led to additional fields and disciplines. History got related to politics, psychology to the history of a concept and then to biology, anthropology to social studies, and philosophy to history – to name only a few of many connections.

Everything around us is intertwined, and it only broadens our perspective to read from every discipline and field about a certain topic.

We should not forget to incorporate fiction. Novels, plays, and poems are all written by authors in a certain period in history about a group of people going through different experiences. The stories can be as useful as any other book; you just need to learn to pick the right book about your chosen topic. Maybe it is a book written from a particular era you're interested in, or detailing a certain location at some point in history. It might discuss a political topic or a social aspect we are interested in. It might tell the story of a character in pursuit of love, happiness, wealth, fame, or truth – all of which can be your topic of research.

Pinpoint a subject of interest, find a few books to read that discuss it, and make up your mind about it. Become enlightened by reading more and reading better.

William Shakespeare

We cannot end a good book about reading without an excerpt from Shakespeare. Why Shakespeare? Because he examined universal topics in his plays and sonnets. He discussed human beings and their feelings, and as readers, we are humans with feelings. You might have read Shakespeare before and loved it, or you might have feared Shakespeare and struggled to understand him since high school.

We'd like to end the book about reading by reading a part chosen from Shakespeare's play *Twelfth Night, or What You Will* [4]. Whether you have read the play or not, you should relate to the below excerpt; if you've ever had your heart broken, you must relate to that feeling of hurt, anger, and suffering. You must have thought about revenge because of that pain and ways to do so. None other than Shakespeare can articulate better those feelings in words.

We end our book with this poetic feeling, so that you can revisit it from time to time, and feel the emotions expressed within – for there is no better way to read a poem than to re-read and experience it all over again.

Come away, come away, death,

And in sad cypress let me be laid.

Fly away, fly away, breath;

I am slain by a fair cruel maid.

My shroud of white, stuck all with yew,

O, prepare it!

My part of death, no one so true

Did share it.

Not a flower, not a flower sweet,

On my black coffin let there be strown.

Not a friend, not a friend greet

My poor corpse, where my bones shall be thrown.

A thousand thousand sighs to save,

Lay me, O, where

Sad true lover never find my grave,

To weep there!

Twelfth Night by William Shakespeare

CONCLUSION - GIVING IT A TRY

Brandon has always had a crush on Isabelle. She is a stunning young woman with an elegance that swept him off his feet. They've been working together for about a year and he has always wished he had the courage to ask her out, but never finds the right moment.

One day, he hears her asking if someone has some free time during the weekend; she's moving and wants help packing. Their eyes meet, and she approaches him. "Are you free this weekend, Brandon? I know it's a lot to ask, but I really need help. I would never forget it!"

This is his chance to get to know her better and spend some time together outside of the office. Of course, he is free! He disregards any plans he has that weekend and meets with her to help her pack. They start with her living room, which looked more like a library to him.

"Did you read all of these?" asks Brandon as he was closing the fourth cardboard box filled with books.

"Most of them, yes. I still have a few on my list before going to the next visit to the bookstore."

He stands up, getting ready to fill up another box, and starts going over the titles: *Madame Bovary*; *Virginia Woolf: A writer's diary*; *The Stranger*; *The Return of the Ainu: Cultural mobilization and the practice of ethnicity in Japan*; *Things Fall Apart*; *The Phenomenology of Spirit*. He is overwhelmed.

"What kinds of books do you read?" he asks, pondering the titles.

"Oh, everything! I love to learn about every aspect of life, get to know about every culture, get lost in the worlds of different tales, travel through space and time, and contemplate various ideas," she answers with a smile.

"Do you understand all of them? I couldn't understand most of the titles!" asks Brandon in bewilderment.

She laughs and says, "Understanding a book is a process. If you get your mind to it, you'll not only understand, you'll enjoy diving deep into the best of human intellect!"

They keep discussing books all day long while packing them. This is a topic that Isabelle can talk for hours about. She tells her companion about the new ideas she comes across when reading, and how it brings her new insight about the world. She explains the main ideas of a few books that catch his attention, as they finish putting her precious collection in the boxes.

As Brandon heads back home, he passes by a bookstore, thinking about Isabelle, her house filled with books, the ideas she shared with him, and the enchantment that engulfed her. He looks at the books through the windows, and wonders about that process of understanding books. He walks in, willing to give it a try.

This book is for the ones willing to give reading a try; for the ones willing to question what they read, and look for the answers; for the ones willing to converse with the authors, and make the books they read their own. Books belong to their writers as much as they do to you.

Even in today's world, we still need to read books, and it would be a waste not to make the most out of them. To do so, we need to understand them better by being an active reader and knowing that reading can have different goals. A book has much to teach us if one is willing to learn and give it a try. Reading better comes gradually, and with every new level of reading that you accomplish, you will become more proficient and be able to understand better.

In every book you read, you get to have the last word and your interpretation brings meaning to that book. We have discussed how to achieve all of that within those pages, and we also went over a few strategies to help us remember better what we read and build up our vocabulary. We also got to know the ways to read different kinds of books.

Now that you've concluded reading this book, it is time to venture to give other books a try with a fresh set of eyes.

We hope that you have found in these pages the tools to help you make the most out of your reading.

Read on and enjoy!

OVER 10,000 PEOPLE HAVE ALREADY SUBSCRIBED. DID YOU TAKE YOUR CHANCE YET?

In general, around 50% of the people who start reading do not finish a book. You are the exception, and we are happy you took the time.

To honor this, we invite you to join our exclusive Thinknetic newsletter. You cannot find this subscription link anywhere else on the web but in our books!

Upon signing up, you'll receive two of our most popular bestselling books, highly acclaimed by readers like yourself. We sell copies of these books daily, but you will receive them as a gift. Additionally, you'll gain access to two transformative short sheets and enjoy complimentary access to all our upcoming e-books, completely free of charge!

This offer and our newsletter are free; you can unsubscribe anytime.

Here's everything you get:

✓ Critical Thinking For Complex Issues eBook **($9.99 Value)**
✓ The Intelligent Reader's Guide To Reading eBook **($9.99 Value)**
✓ Break Your Thinking Patterns Sheet **($4.99 Value)**
✓ Flex Your Wisdom Muscle Sheet **($4.99 Value)**
✓ All our upcoming eBooks **($199.80* Value)**

Total Value: $229.76

Go to thinknetic.net for the offer!

(Or simply scan the code with your camera)

SCAN ME

*If you download 20 of our books for free, this would equal a value of
199.80$

THE TEAM BEHIND THINKNETIC

Michael Meisner, Founder and CEO

When Michael got into publishing books on Amazon, he found that his favorite topic - the thinking process and its results, is tackled in a much too complex and unengaging way. Thus, he set himself up to make his ideal a reality: books that are informative, entertaining, and can help people achieve success by thinking things through.

This ideal became his passion and profession. He built a team of like-minded people and is in charge of the strategic part and brand orientation, as he continues to improve and extend his business.

Diana Spoiala, Publishing Manager

From idea to print, there is a process that involves research, outlining, writing, editing, and design. Diana oversees all stages of this process and ensures the quality of each book. She is also the head behind our weekly newsletter, curating and creating content that complements Thinknetic's published works.

Claire M. Umali, Publishing Co-Manager

Crafting books is collaborative work, and keeping everyone on the same page is an essential task. Claire coordinates every member of the team involved in crafting Thinknetic's books, attending to queries and providing support wherever needed. In her free time, she writes reviews online and likes to bother her cats.

Wedad Naji Khoder, Writer

Wedad is a writer with an MA in English Lit and a Fine Arts degree. She has an eclectic background in writing, drawing, teaching, marketing, and sales, all of which are combined with a passion for words.

Alfonso E. Padilla, Content Editor

Mexican editor with a background in journalism. Alfonso takes pride in his curiosity and cares deeply about learning. True to his formation, he prioritizes solid research and sources when reviewing texts. His main tool for editing is the use of questions.

Sandra Agarrat, Language Editor

Sandra Wall Agarrat is an experienced freelance academic editor/proofreader, writer, and researcher. Sandra holds graduate degrees in Public Policy and International Relations. Her portfolio of projects includes books, dissertations, theses, scholarly articles, and grant proposals.

Michelle Olarte, Researcher

Michelle conducts extensive research and constructs thorough outlines that substantiate Thinknetic's book structure. She graduated from Communication Studies with high honors. Her works include screenplays, book editing, book advertisements, and magazine articles.

Ralph Escarda, Layout Designer

Ralph completes our books' journey to getting published, making sure that every book is properly formatted. His love for books prevails in his artistic preoccupations. He is an avid reader of non-fictional books and an advocate of self-improvement through education. He dedicates his spare time to doing portraits and sports.

REFERENCES

1. Are Books Useless In A Digital World?

1. Birkerts, S. (2013). Reading in a digital age: Notes on why the novel and the Internet are opposites, and why the latter both undermines the former and makes it more necessary. In Socken, P. (Ed.), *The edge of precipice: Why read literature in the digital age?* (pp. 27-41). McGill-Queen's University Press.
2. Birkerts, S. (2013). Reading in a digital age: Notes on why the novel and the Internet are opposites, and why the latter both undermines the former and makes it more necessary. In Socken, P. (Ed.), *The edge of precipice: Why read literature in the digital age?* (pp. 27-41). McGill-Queen's University Press.
3. Carr, N. (2010). *The shallows: How the internet is changing the way we think, read and remember.* Atlantic Books.
4. Colom, R., Karama, S., Jung, R., & Haier, R. (2010). Human intelligence and brain networks. *Dialogues In Clinical Neuroscience, 12*(4), 489-501. https://doi.org/10.31887/dcns.2010.12.4/rcolom
5. Vine, B. (2020, February 19). *What the internet is doing to our brains.* BrainWorld. https://brainworldmagazine.com/what-the-internet-is-doing-to-our-brains/#:~:text=Furthermore%20as%20Academic%20Earth%20reports,every%20time%20we%20experience%20it.%E2%80%9D
6. Vine, B. (2020, February 19). *What the internet is doing to our brains.* BrainWorld. https://brainworldmagazine.com/what-the-internet-is-doing-to-our-brains/#:~:text=Furthermore%20as%20Academic%20Earth%20reports,every%20time%20we%20experience%20it.%E2%80%9D
7. Oliver, P. (2012). *Succeeding with your literature review: A handbook for students.* Open University Press.
8. Bloom, H. (2001). *How to read and why.* Simon and Schuster.
9. Facione, P. (1990). Critical thinking: A statement of expert consensus for purposes of educational assessment and instruction (The Delphi Report).
10. Wallace, M., & Wray, A. (2011). *Critical reading and writing for postgraduates* (2nd Ed.). Sage Publications.

11. Fisher, A. (2011). *Critical thinking: An introduction* (2nd Ed.). Cambridge University Press.
12. https://naturalnews.com/039461_Bloomberg_NYC_students_illiterate.html
13. https://www.edweek.org/leadership/opinion-how-new-york-city-is-working-to-improve-students-social-emotional-learning/2018/03

2. Reading For Insight

1. Perry, W. G. (2001). *Harvard report*. Dartmouth College. https://students.dartmouth.edu/academic-skills/sites/students_academic_skills.prod/files/students_academic_skills/wysiwyg/harvard_report_on_reading.pdf
2. Haussamen, B. (1995). The passive-reading fallacy. *Journal of Reading, 38*(5), 378-381. http://www.jstor.org/stable/40033254
3. Adler, M., & Van Doren, C. (1972). How to read a book: The classic guide to intelligent reading. Simon & Schuster.
4. Haussamen, B. (1995). The passive-reading fallacy. *Journal of Reading, 38*(5), 378-381. http://www.jstor.org/stable/40033254
5. Sun, T. (2020). Active versus passive reading: How to read scientific papers?. *National Science Review*, 7(9), 1422-1427. https://doi.org/10.1093/nsr/nwaa130
6. Adler, M., & Van Doren, C. (1972). How to read a book: The classic guide to intelligent reading. Simon & Schuster.
7. Nash-Ditzel, S. (2010). Metacognitive reading strategies can improve self-regulation. *Journal Of College Reading And Learning*, 40(2), 45-63. https://doi.org/10.1080/10790195.2010.10850330
8. Sun, T. (2020). Active versus passive reading: How to read scientific papers?. *National Science Review*, 7(9), 1422-1427. https://doi.org/10.1093/nsr/nwaa130
9. Adler, M., & Van Doren, C. (1972). How to read a book: The classic guide to intelligent reading. Simon & Schuster.
10. Nash-Ditzel, S. (2010). Metacognitive reading strategies can improve self-regulation. *Journal Of College Reading And Learning*, 40(2), 45-63. https://doi.org/10.1080/10790195.2010.10850330
11. https://www.nationalgeographic.com/magazine/article/why-a-placebo-can-workeven-when-you-know-its-fake

3. Don't Just Read

1. Mikulecky, B., & Jeffries, L. (1996). *More reading power*. Addison-Wesley.

2. Department of Education, UK. (2012). *Research evidence on reading for pleasure.* https://assets.publishing.service.gov.uk/government/uploads/system/uploads/attachment_data/file/284286/reading_for_pleasure.pdf

3. Adler, M., & Van Doren, C. (1972). How to read a book: The classic guide to intelligent reading. Simon & Schuster.

4. Adler, M., & Van Doren, C. (1972). How to read a book: The classic guide to intelligent reading. Simon & Schuster.

5. Seattle Times staff & news services. (2022). Coronavirus daily news updates, May 19: What to know today about COVID-19 in the Seattle area, Washington state and the world. *The Seattle Times.* https://www.seattletimes.com/seattle-news/health/coronavirus-daily-news-updates-may-19-what-to-know-today-about-covid-19-in-the-seattle-area-washington-state-and-the-world-2/

6. Department of Education, UK. (2012). *Research evidence on reading for pleasure.* https://assets.publishing.service.gov.uk/government/uploads/system/uploads/attachment_data/file/284286/reading_for_pleasure.pdf

7. Adler, M., & Van Doren, C. (1972). How to read a book: The classic guide to intelligent reading. Simon & Schuster.

8. Adler, M., & Van Doren, C. (1972). How to read a book: The classic guide to intelligent reading. Simon & Schuster.

9. Wallace, M., & Wray, A. (2011). *Critical reading and writing for postgraduates* (2nd ed.). Sage Publications.

10. Wallace, M., & Wray, A. (2011). *Critical reading and writing for postgraduates* (2nd ed.). Sage Publications.

11. Harvey, S., & Goudvis, A. (2007). *Strategies that work: Teaching comprehension for understanding and engagement* (2nd ed.). Portland: Stenhouse Publishers.

12. Adler, M., & Van Doren, C. (1972). How to read a book: The classic guide to intelligent reading. Simon & Schuster.

13. Smith, B.D., & Morris, L. (2007). *Breaking through college reading* (12th ed.). Pearson/Longman

14. https://www.nature.com/articles/s41392-020-00243-2#citeas

4. Read to Discover

1. Adler, M., & Van Doren, C. (1972). How to read a book: The classic guide to intelligent reading. Simon & Schuster.

2. Harvey, S., & Goudvis, A. (2007). *Strategies that work: Teaching comprehension for understanding and engagement* (2nd ed.). Portland: Stenhouse Publishers.

3. Adler, M., & Van Doren, C. (1972). How to read a book: The classic guide to intelligent reading. Simon & Schuster.
4. Kotee, T., & Nguyen, C. (2021, July 16). Instruction vs. discovery learning in the business classroom. *AACSB*. https://www.aacsb.edu/insights/articles/2021/07/instruction-vs-discovery-learning-in-the-business-classroom#:~:text=Discovery%20learning%20is%20an%20inquiry,%E2%80%94essentially%20%E2%80%9Cinstructionless%E2%80%9D%20learning
5. Adler, M., & Van Doren, C. (1972). How to read a book: The classic guide to intelligent reading. Simon & Schuster.
6. Kotee, T., & Nguyen, C. (2021, July 16). Instruction vs. discovery learning in the business classroom. *AACSB*. https://www.aacsb.edu/insights/articles/2021/07/instruction-vs-discovery-learning-in-the-business-classroom#:~:text=Discovery%20learning%20is%20an%20inquiry,%E2%80%94essentially%20%E2%80%9Cinstructionless%E2%80%9D%20learning
7. Adler, M., & Van Doren, C. (1972). How to read a book: The classic guide to intelligent reading. Simon & Schuster.
8. Adler, M., & Van Doren, C. (1972). How to read a book: The classic guide to intelligent reading. Simon & Schuster.
9. Harvey, S., & Goudvis, A. (2007). *Strategies that work: Teaching comprehension for understanding and engagement* (2nd ed.). Portland: Stenhouse Publishers.
10. Adler, M., & Van Doren, C. (1972). How to read a book: The classic guide to intelligent reading. Simon & Schuster.
11. Cuesta College (n.d.). *Levels of Comprehension*. Cuesta College. Retrieved October 6, 2022, from https://www.cuesta.edu/student/resources/ssc/study_guides/reading_comp/302_read_levels.html
12. Duke, N., & Pearson, P. (2002). Effective practices for developing reading comprehension. *What Research Has to Say About Reading Instruction*, 205-242. DOI: 10.1598/0872071774.10
13. Kent State University Writing Commons. *Three levels comprehension guide for active reading.* https://www-s3-live.kent.edu/s3fs-root/s3fs-public/file/Three%20Level%20Comprehension%20Guide%20for%20Active%20Reading.pdf
14. Duke, N., & Pearson, P. (2002). Effective practices for developing reading comprehension. *What Research Has to Say About Reading Instruction*, 205-242. DOI: 10.1598/0872071774.10
15. Cuesta College (n.d.). *Levels of Comprehension*. Cuesta College. Retrieved October 6, 2022, from https://www.cuesta.edu/student/resources/ssc/study_guides/reading_comp/302_read_levels.html
16. Cuesta College (n.d.). *Levels of Comprehension*. Cuesta College.

Retrieved October 6, 2022, from https://www.cuesta.edu/student/resources/ssc/study_guides/reading_comp/302_read_levels.html

17. Kent State University Writing Commons. *Three levels comprehension guide for active reading.* https://www-s3-live.kent.edu/s3fs-root/s3fs-public/file/Three%20Level%20Comprehension%20Guide%20for%20Active%20Reading.pdf

18. Duke, N., & Pearson, P. (2002). Effective practices for developing reading comprehension. *What Research Has to Say About Reading Instruction,* 205-242. DOI: 10.1598/0872071774.10

19. Cuesta College (n.d.). *Levels of Comprehension.* Cuesta College. Retrieved October 6, 2022, from https://www.cuesta.edu/student/resources/ssc/study_guides/reading_comp/302_read_levels.html

20. Kent State University Writing Commons. *Three levels comprehension guide for active reading.* https://www-s3-live.kent.edu/s3fs-root/s3fs-public/file/Three%20Level%20Comprehension%20Guide%20for%20Active%20Reading.pdf

21. Cuesta College (n.d.). *Levels of Comprehension.* Cuesta College. Retrieved October 6, 2022, from https://www.cuesta.edu/student/resources/ssc/study_guides/reading_comp/302_read_levels.html

22. Duke, N., & Pearson, P. (2002). Effective practices for developing reading comprehension. *What Research Has to Say About Reading Instruction,* 205-242. DOI: 10.1598/0872071774.10

23. Kent State University Writing Commons. *Three levels comprehension guide for active reading.* https://www-s3-live.kent.edu/s3fs-root/s3fs-public/file/Three%20Level%20Comprehension%20Guide%20for%20Active%20Reading.pdf

24. https://public.wsu.edu/~campbelld/engl494/winterdreams.pdf

25. Wagner-Martin, L. (2016). Writing "naturally in sentences": The joys of reading F. Scott Fitzgerald. *The F. Scott Fitzgerald Review, 14*(1), 215–228. https://doi.org/10.5325/fscotfitzrevi.14.1.0215

5. From Basics To Expertise

1. Adler, M., & Van Doren, C. (1972). How to read a book: The classic guide to intelligent reading. Simon & Schuster.

2. McNamara, D. S. (Ed.). (2007). *Reading comprehension strategies: Theories, interventions, and technologies.* Psychology Press.

3. McNamara, D. S. (Ed.). (2007). *Reading comprehension strategies: Theories, interventions, and technologies.* Psychology Press.

4. Adler, M., & Van Doren, C. (1972). How to read a book: The classic guide to intelligent reading. Simon & Schuster.

5. Adler, M., & Van Doren, C. (1972). How to read a book: The classic guide to intelligent reading. Simon & Schuster.
6. McNamara, D. S. (Ed.). (2007). *Reading comprehension strategies: Theories, interventions, and technologies.* Psychology Press.
7. McNamara, D. S. (Ed.). (2007). *Reading comprehension strategies: Theories, interventions, and technologies.* Psychology Press.
8. Adler, M., & Van Doren, C. (1972). How to read a book: The classic guide to intelligent reading. Simon & Schuster.
9. Adler, M., & Van Doren, C. (1972). How to read a book: The classic guide to intelligent reading. Simon & Schuster.
10. Adler, M., & Van Doren, C. (1972). How to read a book: The classic guide to intelligent reading. Simon & Schuster.
11. Lewis, N. (1958). *How to read better and faster.* Crowell.
12. Adler, M., & Van Doren, C. (1972). How to read a book: The classic guide to intelligent reading. Simon & Schuster.
13. Adler, M., & Van Doren, C. (1972). How to read a book: The classic guide to intelligent reading. Simon & Schuster.
14. Wimsatt, W.K., & Beardsley, M. C. (1946). The intentional fallacy. *The Sewanee Review,* 54(3), 468-488.
15. Plato, B. (1977). *Republic. Book I.* Bradda Books.
16. Wimsatt, W.K., & Beardsley, M. C. (1946). The intentional fallacy. *The Sewanee Review,* 54(3), 468-488.
17. Adler, M., & Van Doren, C. (1972). How to read a book: The classic guide to intelligent reading. Simon & Schuster.
18. Foucault, M. (2003). *Madness and civilization* (2nd ed.). Routledge.
19. Adler, M., & Van Doren, C. (1972). How to read a book: The classic guide to intelligent reading. Simon & Schuster.
20. Adler, M., & Van Doren, C. (1972). How to read a book: The classic guide to intelligent reading. Simon & Schuster.

6. The Art Of Literary Interpretations

1. Nguyen, T. (2013). What blue curtains mean: The extent of a reasonable interpretation. https://ucbcluj.org/2013/03/11/what-blue-curtains-mean-the-extent-of-a-reasonable-interpretation/.
2. Castle, G. (2013). *The literary theory handbook.* Wiley Blackwell.
3. Castle, G. (2013). *The literary theory handbook.* Wiley Blackwell.
4. Castle, G. (2013). *The literary theory handbook.* Wiley Blackwell.
5. Montgomery, M., Durant, A., Furniss, T., & Mills, S. (2006). *Ways of reading* (3rd ed.). Routledge.
6. Nguyen, T. (2013). What blue curtains mean: The extent of a

reasonable interpretation. https://ucbcluj.org/2013/03/11/what-blue-curtains-mean-the-extent-of-a-reasonable-interpretation/.

7. Van Teslaar, J. S. (1912). Psychoanalysis: A review of current literature. *The American Journal of Psychology*, *23*(2), 309–327. https://doi.org/10.2307/1412845

8. Lidz, T. (1975). *Hamlet's enemy: Madness and myth in Hamlet*. Basic Books.

9. Lewis, R. (2020). *Hamlet and the vision of darkness*. Princeton University Press.

10. Montgomery, M., Durant, A., Furniss, T., & Mills, S. (2006). *Ways of reading* (3rd ed.). Routledge.

11. Nguyen, T. (2013). What blue curtains mean: The extent of a reasonable interpretation. https://ucbcluj.org/2013/03/11/what-blue-curtains-mean-the-extent-of-a-reasonable-interpretation/.

12. Montgomery, M., Durant, A., Furniss, T., & Mills, S. (2006). *Ways of reading* (3rd ed.). Routledge.

13. Montgomery, M., Durant, A., Furniss, T., & Mills, S. (2006). *Ways of reading* (3rd ed.). Routledge.

14. Montgomery, M., Durant, A., Furniss, T., & Mills, S. (2006). *Ways of reading* (3rd ed.). Routledge.

15. Brantlinger, P. (2007). Kipling's "The white man's burden" and its afterlives. *English Literature in Transition*, 1880-1920 50(2), 172-191. DOI:10.1353/elt.2007.0017.

16. https://shec.ashp.cuny.edu/items/show/505

7. After Reading Comes Remembering

1. Ranpura, A. (2013, March 12). *How we remember and why we forget*. Brain Connection. https://brainconnection.brainhq.com/2013/03/12/how-we-remember-and-why-we-forget/

2. Kindleberger, C. P. (1986). *The world in depression, 1929-1939* (2nd ed.). University of California Press.

3. Ranpura, A. (2013, March 12). *How we remember and why we forget*. Brain Connection. https://brainconnection.brainhq.com/2013/03/12/how-we-remember-and-why-we-forget/

4. Wong, L. (2003). *Essential study skills*. Houghton Mifflin Co.

5. Wong, L. (2003). *Essential study skills*. Houghton Mifflin Co.

6. Kindleberger, C. P. (1986). *The world in depression, 1929-1939* (2nd ed.). University of California Press.

7. Chesla, E. (2000). *Read better, remember more* (2nd ed.). Learning Express.

8. Chesla, E. (2000). *Read better, remember more* (2nd ed.). Learning Express.
9. McKay, B., McKay, K. (2021, May 1). *The best way to retain what you read.* The Art of Manliness. https://www.artofmanliness.com/living/reading/the-best-way-to-retain-what-you-read/
10. Nast, J. (2006). *Idea mapping: How to access your hidden brain power, learn faster, remember more, and achieve success in business.* John Wiley & Sons.
11. Kudelic, R., Konecki, M., & Maleković, M. (2011). Mind map generator software model with text mining algorithm. *Proceedings of the International Conference on Information Technology Interfaces, ITI.* DOI:10.13140/RG.2.1.1455.5601
12. Nast, J. (2006). *Idea mapping: How to access your hidden brain power, learn faster, remember more, and achieve success in business.* John Wiley & Sons.
13. Kudelic, R., Konecki, M., & Maleković, M. (2011). Mind map generator software model with text mining algorithm. *Proceedings of the International Conference on Information Technology Interfaces, ITI.* DOI:10.13140/RG.2.1.1455.5601
14. Serrat, O. (2009). *Drawing mind maps.* Asian Development Bank. https://www.think-asia.org/bitstream/handle/11540/2738/drawing-mind-maps.pdf
15. Nast, J. (2006). *Idea mapping: How to access your hidden brain power, learn faster, remember more, and achieve success in business.* John Wiley & Sons.
16. https://books.google.com.lb/books?hl=en&lr=&id=BprUZfxswH4C&oi=fnd&pg=PR11&dq=depression&ots=cjjiZcLRWU&sig=TasKpFEHReDdwgBuR_xlxvM5kiU&redir_esc=y#v=onepage&q&f=false

8. Mastering Vocabulary

1. Paris, S. (2005). Reinterpreting the development of reading skills. *Reading Research Quarterly, 40 (2)*, 184-202. https://doi.org/10.1598/RRQ.40.2.3
2. State of Victoria, Department of Education and Training. (2021). *Literacy teaching toolkit: Vocabulary.* State of Victoria. https://www.education.vic.gov.au/school/teachers/teachingresources/discipline/english/literacy/readingviewing/Pages/litfocusvocab.aspx#:~:text=Focussing%20on%20vocabulary%20is%20use-ful,%2C%20comprehension%2C%20and%20also%20fluency
3. State of Victoria, Department of Education and Training. (2021). *Literacy teaching toolkit: Vocabulary.* State of Victoria. https://www.education.vic.gov.au/school/teachers/teachingresources/discipline/english/literacy/readingviewing/Pages/litfocusvocab.

aspx#:~:text=Focussing%20on%20vocabulary%20is%20useful,%2C%20comprehension%2C%20and%20also%20fluency

4. Hughes, G. (2000). *A history of English words*. Wiley-Blackwell.
5. Hughes, G. (2000). *A history of English words*. Wiley-Blackwell.
6. State of Victoria, Department of Education and Training. (2021). *Literacy teaching toolkit: Vocabulary*. State of Victoria. https://www.education.vic.gov.au/school/teachers/teachingresources/discipline/english/literacy/readingviewing/Pages/litfocusvocab.aspx#:~:text=Focussing%20on%20vocabulary%20is%20useful,%2C%20comprehension%2C%20and%20also%20fluency
7. Jenkins, J. R., Stein, M. L., & Wysocki, K. (1984). Learning Vocabulary Through Reading. *American Educational Research Journal, 21*(4), 767–787. https://doi.org/10.3102/00028312021004767
8. Jenkins, J. R., Stein, M. L., & Wysocki, K. (1984). Learning Vocabulary Through Reading. *American Educational Research Journal, 21*(4), 767–787. https://doi.org/10.3102/00028312021004767
9. Nagy, W. E., & Anderson, R. C. (1982). *The numbers of words in printed school English* (Tech. Rep. No. 253). Champaign: University of Illinois, Center for the Study of Reading. https://core.ac.uk/download/pdf/4826231.pdf
10. Carter, R., & McCarthy, M. (2014). *Vocabulary and language teaching*. Routledge.
11. Adams, S. J. (1982). Scripts and the recognition of unfamiliar vocabulary: Enhancing second language reading skills. *The Modern Language Journal, 66*(2), 155–159. https://doi.org/10.2307/326384
12. Carter, R., & McCarthy, M. (2014). *Vocabulary and language teaching*. Routledge.
13. Adams, S. J. (1982). Scripts and the recognition of unfamiliar vocabulary: Enhancing second language reading skills. *The Modern Language Journal, 66*(2), 155–159. https://doi.org/10.2307/326384
14. Carter, R., & McCarthy, M. (2014). *Vocabulary and language teaching*. Routledge.
15. Carter, R., & McCarthy, M. (2014). *Vocabulary and language teaching*. Routledge.
16. Carter, R., & McCarthy, M. (2014). *Vocabulary and language teaching*. Routledge.
17. Prince, P. (1996). Second language vocabulary learning: The role of context versus translations as a function of proficiency. *The Modern Language Journal, 80*(4), 478-493. https://doi.org/10.2307/329727
18. https://books.google.com.lb/books?id=ZkThXFvOKZYC&printsec=frontcover&dq=thomas+hardy+return+of+the+native&hl=en&sa=X&ved=2ahUKEwjE7q7Ixar5AhUIhc4BHdhDD9kQuwV6BAgIEAc#v=onepage&q&f=false

9. Specialized Reading Techniques

1. A&M-Central Texas University Library. (2022, January 13). *Children's genre list for teacher education: Nonfiction expository.* https://tamuct.libguides.com/c.php?g=439801&p= 3927342#:~:text=Non%2DFiction%20Expository%20%E2%80%93%20These%20are,works%2C%20why%20-something%20is%20important

2. Adler, M., & Van Doren, C. (1972). *How to read a book: The classic guide to intelligent reading.* Simon & Schuster.

3. Prychitko, D. L. (2004, September 6). *The nature and significance of Marx's: Capital: A critique of political economy.* Econlib. https://www.econlib.org/library/Columns/y2004/PrychitkoMarx.html

4. Dobson, T., Michura, P., Ruecker, S., Brown, M., & Rodriguez, O. (2011). Interactive Visualizations of Plot in Fiction. *Visible Language,* 45(3).

5. Wasow, B. (2021, May 23). *Karl Marx and Milton Friedman: What they got right.* The Globalist. https://www.theglobalist.com/karl-marx-and-milton-friedman-capitalism-communism-ideologies/

6. Adler, M., & Van Doren, C. (1972). *How to read a book: The classic guide to intelligent reading.* Simon & Schuster.

7. Adler, M., & Van Doren, C. (1972). *How to read a book: The classic guide to intelligent reading.* Simon & Schuster.

8. Dobson, T., Michura, P., Ruecker, S., Brown, M., & Rodriguez, O. (2011). Interactive Visualizations of Plot in Fiction. *Visible Language,* 45(3).

9. Adler, M., & Van Doren, C. (1972). *How to read a book: The classic guide to intelligent reading.* Simon & Schuster.

10. Franco, D.J. (2006). What we about when we talk about Beloved. *MFS Modern Fiction Studies, 52*(2), 415-439. https://doi.org/10.1353/mfs.2006.0045

11. Adler, M., & Van Doren, C. (1972). *How to read a book: The classic guide to intelligent reading.* Simon & Schuster.

12. Adler, M., & Van Doren, C. (1972). *How to read a book: The classic guide to intelligent reading.* Simon & Schuster.

13. Arnold, M. (2014). *Essays in criticism: The study of poetry* (S. S. Sheridan, Ed.). Literary Licensing. (Original work published 1896).

14. Adler, M., & Van Doren, C. (1972). *How to read a book: The classic guide to intelligent reading.* Simon & Schuster.

15. Adler, M., & Van Doren, C. (1972). *How to read a book: The classic guide to intelligent reading.* Simon & Schuster.

16. Goldberg, T., & Savenije, G. M. (2018). Teaching controversial historical issues. *The Wiley international handbook of history teaching and learning*, 503-526. https://doi.org/10.1002/9781119100812.ch19

17. Adler, M., & Van Doren, C. (1972). *How to read a book: The classic guide to intelligent reading.* Simon & Schuster.

18. Adler, M., & Van Doren, C. (1972). *How to read a book: The classic guide to intelligent reading.* Simon & Schuster.

19. Groseclose, T., & Milyo, J. (2005). A measure of media bias. *The Quarterly Journal of Economics, 120*(4), 1191-1237. http://www.jstor.org/stable/25098770

20. Adler, M., & Van Doren, C. (1972). *How to read a book: The classic guide to intelligent reading.* Simon & Schuster.

21. Repko, A.F, Szostak R., & Buchberger, M. P. (2016). *Introduction to interdisciplinary studies* (2nd Ed.). Sage.

22. Adler, M., & Van Doren, C. (1972). *How to read a book: The classic guide to intelligent reading.* Simon & Schuster.

23. Helmenstine, A. M. (2020, February 18). *Six steps of the scientific method.* ThoughtCo. https://www.thoughtco.com/steps-of-the-scientific-method-p2-606045

24. Whitehead, A. N. (2017). *An introduction to mathematics.* Courier Dover Publications.

25. Adler, M., & Van Doren, C. (1972). *How to read a book: The classic guide to intelligent reading.* Simon & Schuster.

26. Whitehead, A. N. (2017). *An introduction to mathematics.* Courier Dover Publications.

27. Adler, M., & Van Doren, C. (1972). *How to read a book: The classic guide to intelligent reading.* Simon & Schuster.

28. Adler, M., & Van Doren, C. (1972). *How to read a book: The classic guide to intelligent reading.* Simon & Schuster.

29. Adler, M., & Van Doren, C. (1972). *How to read a book: The classic guide to intelligent reading.* Simon & Schuster.

30. Fassio, A. (2017, February 28). How to read philosophy (a step-by-step guide for confused students!). *The University of Edinburgh, School of Philosophy, Psychology, and Language Sciences: my PPLS Journey, Student Blog.* https://www.blogs.ppls.ed.ac.uk/2017/02/28/read-philosophy-step-step-guide-confused-students/

31. Adler, M., & Van Doren, C. (1972). *How to read a book: The classic guide to intelligent reading.* Simon & Schuster.

32. Chignell, A., & Pereboom, D. (Fall 2020 Edition). Natural theology and natural religion. In E.N. Zalta (Ed.), *The Stanford Encyclopedia of Philosophy.* Metaphysics Research Lab, Stanford University https://plato.stanford.edu/archives/fall2020/entries/natural-theology/

33. Adler, M., & Van Doren, C. (1972). *How to read a book: The classic guide to intelligent reading.* Simon & Schuster.
34. Adler, M., & Van Doren, C. (1972). *How to read a book: The classic guide to intelligent reading.* Simon & Schuster.

10. Evaluate Your Reading Progress

1. Cynthia Turner Camp, department of English, Franklin College of Arts & Sciences (n.d.). *Guide to Reading Middle English.* University of Georgia. Retrieved October 6, 2022, from https://faculty.franklin.uga.edu/ctcamp/resources/reading-middle-english
2. Malory, T. (1889). *Le Morte D'Arthur* (W. Caxton, & H. O. Sommer, Eds.). London: David Nutt. (Original work published 1485). https://quod.lib.umich.edu/cgi/t/text/text-idx?c=cme;idno=MaloryWks2
3. Malory, T. (2009). *Le Morte D'Arthur, volume I: King Arthur and of his noble knights of the round table* (W. Caxton, Ed.). (Original work published 1485). https://www.gutenberg.org/files/1251/1251-h/1251-h.htm#chap05
4. Shakespeare, W. (1908). *Twelfth night, or what you will.* Cassell & Company.

DISCLAIMER

The information contained in this book and its components is meant to serve as a comprehensive collection of strategies that the author of this book has done research about. Summaries, strategies, tips and tricks are only recommendations by the author, and reading this book will not guarantee that one's results will exactly mirror the author's results.

The author of this book has made all reasonable efforts to provide current and accurate information for the readers of this book. The author and their associates will not be held liable for any unintentional errors or omissions that may be found.

The material in the book may include information by third parties. Third party materials are comprised of opinions expressed by their owners. As such, the author of this book does not assume responsibility or liability for any third party material or opinions.

Made in the USA
Monee, IL
04 December 2024

72354580R00135